open

LOVE, SEX,

and LIFE

in an

OPEN MARRIAGE

JENNY BLOCK

SEAL PRESS

open

LOVE, SEX, *and* LIFE *in an* OPEN MARRIAGE

Published by Seal Press

A Member of Perseus Books Group

1700 Fourth Street

Berkeley, CA 94710

Library of Congress Cataloging-in-Publication Data

Block, Jenny.

Open : love, sex, and life in an open marriage / by Jenny Block. --

2nd ed.

p. cm.

Includes bibliographical references.

ISBN-13: 978-1-58005-275-7

ISBN-10: 1-58005-275-4

1. Open marriage. 2. Marriage. 3. Communication in marriage. I.

Title.

HQ536.B595 2009

306.84--dc22

2008040700

The author has changed some names, places, and recognizable details to protect the privacy of friends and family members mentioned in the book.

Interior design by Tabitha Lahr

Printed in the United States of America

Distributed by Publishers Group West

For J

contents

prologue

this is a story about a girl who grew up
believing what many girls believe—that one day she would fall
in love with the man of her dreams, marry him, have kids, and
live happily ever after. Yet as she grew older, all she felt was
confused. The messages she was getting—from her parents, her
friends, her school, the media—about looks and love and sex and
relationships all seemed to be pointing in different directions.

When she was seventeen, she lost her virginity to a guy who
told her that she was responsible for her own orgasms. She set off
for college feeling confident about her sexuality; she had several
relationships and many lovers, and she was happy.

Then she met a nice guy whom she thought she could love. He
was what she imagined she had always wanted—someone kind

and smart, who would love her and take care of her. The summer they started dating, she slept with another woman, but then decided she was ready to settle down. He said "I do" and she said "I do," and for a while they were happy. Then they had a baby and their sex life plummeted, and she soon realized that her sex drive was far greater than his. And so she had an affair. She told him about it, and they decided they'd work on their marriage. After all, what else was there to do?

She made a pact with herself to try to be what was expected of her. They moved to a planned community, and she baked brownies and volunteered at her daughter's school. She hosted happy hours and wore sundresses. But she couldn't keep it up. Her marriage couldn't last the way it was. She thought maybe she had married the wrong guy, or that maybe she was a lesbian. She thought perhaps she just needed to have lovers outside of her marriage. Talking to her husband about what she needed was the only way to figure it out. It was the hardest thing she'd ever have to do, but she had to try.

When they talked about it, she realized that she wanted to show him how they could still be together and love each other and be married—even if they slept with other people. Figuring a threesome would be a good place to start, she invited her best friend to sleep with them. The three of them were together for a while, until it turned out that the friend wanted to sleep only with the husband. And so she asked whether she could sleep with other people, too, and her husband said yes—but a few ground rules needed to be laid out. And so their open marriage began.

Figuring it all out took a lot of talking, but the couple was happy. She experimented here and there when she was out of town. She slept with other people and felt more connected to her husband. She slowly began to accept that she was okay, that her choices were right for her, and that her husband was onboard. And that was all that mattered.

Soon she decided that she wanted to date only women outside her marriage. And it wasn't long before she met a young woman who became her friend, and then her lover. They fell in love and she wondered what that meant, or if it had to mean anything. Was she polyamorous? Was she a lesbian? Was she staying in her marriage for the wrong reasons—for comfort and convenience? In time, though, she realized that having an exclusive girlfriend was part of her larger journey.

It became increasingly clear that open marriage was not what most people think. People thought she was promiscuous, or that she hosted orgies, or that her daughter saw her with other people. Some people thought she and her husband were immoral, and that the only way to live was in a monogamous, heterosexual marriage. Some people thought she was selfish and a bad mother. But she and her husband knew that their marriage looked like most people's marriages—except that they were honest with each other, and they were happier than they'd ever been.

As time went on, she realized that several key elements make a successful open marriage, and though those factors involved the community of people she surrounded herself with, it was mostly about how she chose to act and react, and how to be in her relationship and her own skin. Having come this far, she more than realized that it was never going to be easy. She was always going to need to protect her daughter. Things couldn't always be exactly as she wanted them to be. But she was doing it, and she knew she wasn't alone in her journey.

She finally decided that she didn't need to know what it all meant or where it was all going. What she did know was that everyone is different, so it made sense to her that every marriage might be different. For now, her marriage was working. She had a husband and a girlfriend who loved her, and a daughter who was doing just fine. Why shouldn't they keep on doing what they were doing, she reasoned, and see if they couldn't define for themselves their own happily ever after?

Chapter 1
what's a girl to do?

This is a story about a girl who grew up believing what many girls believe—that one day she would fall in love with the man of her dreams, marry him, have kids, and live happily ever after. Yet as she grew older, all she felt was confused. The messages she was getting—from her parents, her friends, her school, the media—about looks and love and sex and relationships all seemed to be pointing in different directions.

i blame Cinderella. And Barbie, for that matter. Ever since I was a little girl, even though my parents were hippies who pushed the Sunshine Family over Barbie and public television over Disney, I grew up with visions of

Prince Charming and Ken dancing in my head. That vision involved meeting a man, falling in love, knowing he was The One, and then having children. I grew up believing that sex happened within that very specific and societally prescribed realm. And despite not knowing exactly what sex was, I knew it was something that two grownups did *in private* when they loved each other *very much*.

I clung to that ideal, like a lot of young girls do. I played bride and wedding and happily ever after, and I assumed that one day, my perfect man and I would ride off into the sunset and go do that sex thing. The ongoing themes of love and sex and marriage were all included in the same brew, no one idea mutually exclusive from the others.

As I got older and outgrew my princess obsession, like many girls entering adolescence, I simply moved on to other media visions of love and sex and marriage. But they all communicated the same happily ever after message about falling in love and having sex. Occasionally, something would slip out about having sex before marriage, but it was generally assumed that marriage was in your future. Your *near* future. Unless, of course, you were a slut. And no one I knew was striving for that.

I grew up in a liberal household with parents who told me I could do anything I set my mind to, and be anyone I wanted to be. So when my own vision strayed from the clichéd one I was surrounded with, my parents were able to roll with the punches. When I was about eight or nine, I told them, "When I grow up, I'm going to live in a penthouse in New York City, and I'm going to have lots of boyfriends. But I'm never going to get married and I'm never going to have any children and I'm going to be the first woman president of the United States."

"You can be anything you like and live however you like," my mom responded. "But you don't have to make any of those decisions yet. You can change your mind a hundred times before you head out into the world—and even once you do." So you see, I was groomed to think for myself, to be able to dissect the messages I encountered. Perhaps because of this training (or in spite of it), as early as high school, things just didn't seem quite right to me. Every cultural standard that confronted me told me that sex before marriage was bad, that "nice" girls waited until marriage, that virginity was something your future husband expected of you.

Meanwhile, the media was blasting images—yes, even back then—of young girls who exuded sex appeal. Take the famous Calvin Klein ad from 1980 in which fifteen-year-old Brooke Shields purred, "Do you wanna know what comes between me and my Calvins? Nothing." The underlying message was about sex and desirability, and even about her landing a man, despite her ridiculously young age. And wasn't that what I was supposed to be looking for? I was ten years old, and I felt I *had* to look like her. At the same time, Brooke Shields was so distant a creature that it seemed preposterous to imagine myself ever being that seductive.

And yet every time someone said, "Make a wish," that was mine: to be beautiful and sexy enough for men to want me. Forget about intelligence or wit; looking a certain way—sexy but not slutty, beautiful but not unattainable—was how you captured a man and got him to marry you. And although marriage seemed like a far-off concept, the idea of capturing men's attention didn't. I could see it in the ads, in the movies, and at the roller rink, as the girls threw back their feathered locks and shot the boys hanging on the rail at the rink's edge that *look*.

Even then, though, I knew that at some point, some magical switch would turn off and girls would suddenly drop the "Don't you want me?" game, and would just as quickly start playing the role of the "good girl"—to groom themselves into marriage material. I just didn't understand how or when that was supposed to happen. As far as the boys were concerned, at some point they apparently stopped being kitten chasers and started becoming wife wanters. But when? And when were girls supposed to stop wanting to be the object of every boy's desire and start wanting to keep house? I couldn't figure out just what it was that men wanted, and I didn't understand how I could possibly be two different women at the same time.

So, despite being raised by a liberated working mother and an equally feminist father, I still believed that becoming a wife was the one thing above all else that I must shoot for, because it was culturally ingrained in me that it would prove my worth as a human being and a woman. And if you wanted to be a wife, you had to be "wife material," and that meant being virginal, for one. It meant being one of the "good girls," which was defined for me very early on. When I was in junior high and high school, there was still a solid line between nice girls and sluts, and there was no question about who was who. Of course, that delineation hasn't remained quite so clear. Today, nice girls aren't necessarily expected to retain their precious virginity before being labeled sluts, but there's no question that women are still struggling to claim our own sexuality and define for ourselves the sexual roles that continue to be mandated to and for us.

as a culture, we undoubtedly continue

to deal with the problems that arise from conflicting messages about how we're supposed to behave, arguably more so now than when I was growing up. Jessica Valenti, author of *Full Frontal Feminism* and founder of Feministing.com, makes a living keeping her finger on the pulse of young women and the issues they face today. She writes, "Never mind trying to find an authentic sexuality in our fake-orgasm pop culture—it's near impossible to find *anything* that makes sense. There are all of these contradictions in porn/pop culture that blow my mind and make it all the more difficult for young women to find an authentic sexual identity."[1] Ultimately, she concludes, what's expected of women is the impossible.

Her observations echo my very experiences—only fifteen years later. I suppose it's true that the more things change, the more they stay the same.

The media, the church, the politicians—everyone—wants to weigh in, and everyone has something different to say. Women experience a bizarre disconnect in which we are bombarded with images of sex—on television, in films, all over the print media—while receiving cultural messages that girls should strive to retain their purity. "We live in sexually interesting times, meaning a culture which manages to be simultaneously hyper-sexualized and to retain its Puritan underpinnings, in precisely equal proportions," explains Laura Kipnis in her polemic *Against Love*.[2] And it doesn't stop there, because the messages not only are contradictory, but they also place an inexcusable emphasis on girls' bodies. And despite my parents' commitment to fighting that focus, it seeped into our home and my consciousness nevertheless.

I remember an argument my parents had the summer I turned sixteen, about a hot-pink string bikini that I'd bought for myself. Because I had purchased it with my own money, I didn't think I needed my parents' approval. It was just a bathing suit, after all. I had no idea that my purchase would incite such a conflict.

"Debbie, if she can fill the thing out, I don't see what the big deal is," my dad said.

"Very nice," my mother said.

"I'm just teasing," he said.

"I know. It's just not the right time, okay? This is serious."

"I'm sorry. Your mother's right. You know I was just teasing, right?"

"I know."

"It's just, well, I don't know what to say about this stuff."

That was generally how my dad dealt with situations that he desperately wanted to lighten. His jokes didn't always go over well with my mom, especially when they affected my sister and me. It wasn't that our growing up "right" was any less important to my dad; it's just that he could turn anything into a joke, and my mother didn't always see the funny side of things.

My parents went on to argue about the importance of cultivating my sexual confidence versus the likelihood that men would look at me or treat me in a way that they wanted to avoid. "I don't want her boobs hanging out for every pervert to see," my mom told my father. "And besides, it's fashion to her, but it comes across as a statement of sexual availability to others."

"I'm still in the room, Mom," I said.

"I know. I'm sorry."

"Why does everything have to turn into a political discussion?" I asked.

"Because everything *is* political," my mother stated matter-of-factly. I didn't know what she meant then, but I certainly do now. The idea of the personal as political is something I became acutely aware of as a women's studies minor in college, and it's continued to strike me daily ever since. I may be wearing an outfit I like, reading a book that interests me, or watching a movie that I enjoy for some perfectly valid reason, but others may read those actions differently, and I can't walk around with my head in the clouds, acting like that's not the case. There is no reality—there is only perception. My mother's strong feelings were a foundation for my approach to life. Thus, the way I wanted to look, dress, and be perceived became a quandary as I changed from a girl into a woman, trying to balance my mother's ideas with my thoughts and with the messages I was getting from the world around me.

Confounding as this situation was, the messages I received at home could sometimes be as confusing and mixed as the ones I got from the outside world. Although both my mother and my father encouraged my younger sister, Rachel, and me to be aware of the power we held as women, and to realize how important it was to hold our own in a world where our sexuality could be used against us, only our father was willing to talk to us about using it to our benefit. My mother saw that as profoundly antifeminist, a concept I later discovered was a divide that existed within the feminist movement—this idea of what a "real" feminist even looks like. Can a woman be sexy and seductive and still be a feminist? My mom belonged to the camp that believed it wasn't possible, and I definitely belong to the camp that thinks, *Oh, yes indeed.*

As much as my mother wanted us to be aware of the choices we were making, she wasn't always so self-aware when it came to her own decisions. Eating, for example, was a huge issue in our house. My mother always prepared healthy, well-rounded meals, and she expected my sister and me to eat everything on our plates, even the things we loathed. Yet while my father and Rachel and I ate our balanced meal—meat and starch and vegetable—my mother ate a Lean Cuisine. She was trying to maintain her weight for her health, she told us, and I don't doubt that was true. But the message was clear: What we were eating wasn't for weight loss. And she wasn't even eating smaller portions—she was eating something entirely different than we were.

Though my mother primarily emphasized the importance of our being smart and nice, espousing over and over her belief that being pretty didn't matter nearly as much, her concerted effort to lose weight left me feeling conflicted. Wasn't weight not simply connected, but central, to looks? So, despite my mother's explanations, her actions spoke volumes to my sister and me: We shouldn't be focused on looks, but it was okay that *she* was.

I got the message that it's okay to wear a bikini, but only in a vacuum in which reality can't intrude. Being pretty doesn't matter, but you don't want to get fat. Being interested in sex is healthy, but appearing sexually available can be dangerous. And so on. The fact that my mother's values often seemed contradictory baffled me at times, but the signs the universe was sending me were outright dangerous.

The conflicting information that the media, parents, and other sources feed to girls and women leaves us in a space that can feel nearly impossible to navigate: We are told to be sexy, but not too sexy. We are told what is sexy, but wait—only for that minute, actually. We are told what to buy to become sexy—that we *have* to buy things to be sexy—but not slutty. We are told to be able partners, but not too able—because where would we have learned such things? We are told to be willing, but not on the prowl. These contradictions send a lot of women (and men) into a tailspin as we come into our own sexuality.

Glamour magazine has a column in its "Sex & Men" section called "Jake: A Man's Opinion," written by what the magazine calls "a real, live single guy." Jake's September 2007 column was titled "What's Sexy, What's Scary in Bed." He opens the piece talking about a woman who bit his nipple—"hard," he writes. He didn't like it, and he sees this scenario as emblematic of a larger problem: Women are finally taking control and coming into our own sexually, and yet there are men like Jake who take issue with that, who feel as if women's assertiveness (or sluttiness) belongs in a different realm. That behavior is for fake porn girls, not girls Jake wants to date. He blames the web, which he refers to as "that great, sometimes sordid bastion of exhibitionism":

What's a woman to think . . . when she finds out her boyfriend spends hours . . . watching barely legal girls stripping in their bedrooms on YouTube? . . . But that's not necessarily what your boyfriend wants you to do—that's why we have YouTube (and, to a greater extreme, porn).[3]

excuse me? Virgin/whore complex,

anyone? This column, in a mainstream magazine, speaks to the continued way in which we are maligned for our sexuality, yet are still expected to be sexual. "We want a lady in the street but a freak in the bed," Usher sings to his tween and teen fans in his song "Yeah!" Notice that it has nothing to do with what *she* wants—just with what he expects.

Other media "experts" are propagating this balancing act as well. Laura Sessions Stepp, in a *Washington Post* article entitled "Cupid's Broken Arrow," actually suggests that sexually confident women cause impotence in men. One of the young men she interviewed for the article told her, "I know lots of girls for whom nothing is off limits. The pressure on the guys is a huge deal."[4]

A girl willing to do anything? Presumably every guy's fantasy, right? But this college junior is saying that a girl like this can actually feel like too much to deal with, and can prevent a guy from being the ladies' man he might otherwise be. It doesn't matter whether you're talking about college girls or married women—the problem is the same. Women's sexuality must somehow simultaneously exist and not exist. And if men can't perform, we're to blame. Forget confusing—this is just plain not okay.

Unfortunately, when it comes to marriage, this issue doesn't go away; it only becomes magnified. No matter what most people have going on before they get married, it has to stop once they get married. When you date, you have the opportunity to try on different partners: the guy you dabble in S&M with; the girl you play doctor with; the partner who wants you to be a schoolgirl. But once you have a spouse, you're not only left with no outlets, you're also burdened by social definitions of marriage and of who you are expected to be—or become.

Even when sex plays a huge role in the premarital relationship, women are often surprised by the way things change once they become someone's wife and are suddenly expected to be Holly Homemakers, not sex kittens (though we're supposed to still be "desirable" to our husbands, whatever that means). And even if we're working full-time, we must also play the roles of überwife and supermom. We're expected to create an ideal balance, and we're supposed to magically know what that is at any given moment. The truth is, the messages we get are so mixed that it's impossible to know what men want—and *men* probably don't even know what men want.

Even the most liberated couples find themselves falling into traditional patterns once they're married—or even once they're exclusive. Shannon Davis, an assistant professor of sociology at George Mason and the lead author of a 2007 international study entitled "Effects of Union Type on Division of Household Labor: Do Cohabiting Men Really Perform More Housework?" told *USA Today* that "the institution of marriage seems to have an effect on couples that traditionalizes their behavior, even if they view men and women as equals."[5]

A man wants his wife to cook dinner, and he doesn't want her to take over in the bedroom. I am generalizing, of course, but it's a common and dangerous pattern. According to Stephanie Coontz, a professor of history and family studies at Evergreen State College and the author of *Marriage, a History,* "we have all inherited unconscious habits and emotional expectations that perpetuate female disadvantage in marriage."[6] We're raised to believe in an institution, and to follow the rules of that institution, whether or not it counters our own thinking and experiences. It's what we know, and it's what society values.

when I was a teenager, I felt completely

at a loss as I tried to negotiate that space between what was expected of me and how I felt as my own sexual impulses started to kick in. How on earth was I supposed to figure out what men wanted, what I wanted, what was "right" when I couldn't get a straight answer from anyone or anything?

"It's strapless," my mother said when I came out of the dressing room, wearing the dress I had been admiring for weeks, the dress I longed to wear to the homecoming dance the fall of my junior year. "And it's way too sexy."

"Come on, Mom. Everyone's wearing dresses like this. They're in every magazine."

"I'm calling your father," she said. He was already on his way home from work, and we decided to wait at the store for him to arrive.

"Dance with me," my father said when he saw me standing there, wearing the dress of my dreams.

"What?" I asked, stunned.

"Come here. Dance with me." I lifted my arms and put them around my father's neck. We rocked back and forth for a couple of steps, and then he stopped and winked at me. "You pass," he said, dropping his arms and patting my shoulder. My mother and I must have looked completely perplexed. "It stayed up. So as far as I'm concerned, she can wear it."

My mother grumbled, but she let me get the dress. I imagine now that it must have been a confusing time for her as a parent, having been a college student in the '60s, when free love and sex reigned and drugs and rock 'n' roll were de rigueur. And here I was, growing up in this new era of AIDS and television programming that would have been considered scandalous just twenty years earlier.

"The world is changing so fast, Jenny," she would say to me. "I just want to protect you."

"You can't always protect me, Mom."

"I know, but I have to try. It's all too sexy—the clothes, the TV, the music." Strange how those words ring in my ears now, more than twenty years later, as I try to raise a daughter of my own in a world that makes that one look like the Cleavers' by comparison.

This constant theme rang true throughout my upbringing—my parents seemed torn between allowing me to do what I wanted, because only I could know what was best for me, and keeping me under lock and key to protect me from exploring all of the things they had had no experience with during their own upbringings. It was a brave new world, and it made my mother much more nervous than it did my father.

Since I'm writing a book about my own open marriage, it seems imperative to address my parents' marriage and how it impacted my worldview. My parents were married for thirty-three years, but they are no longer together. My dad left my mom when I was thirty, and, though it's hard for me to admit this, he seems happier than I have ever seen him. My mother, on the other hand, continues to struggle with the breakup, even many years later. Looking back, I think my parents loved each other, and I believe they were happy—sometimes. I also know that they disagreed a lot, and that pretty early on, I sensed he was staying in the marriage for my sister's and my sake. He left my mother for a short while when I was twelve, and then came back when my mother was diagnosed with muscular dystrophy and stayed for eighteen more years. But things were the same, possibly even worse. I don't blame either of them for how their relationship played out. As far as I can tell, it was simply a marriage that didn't work.

My parents weren't physically affectionate with each other, although they were with Rachel and me. I distinctly remember the first time I saw my best friend's parents kissing: They looked at each other in a way I'd never seen my own parents act. I was embarrassed at first, wondering, *Is this the way parents are supposed to be?* Once, I saw the dad swat his wife on the butt with a dish towel. She giggled like a little girl and hugged him, the way the couples did on *The Love Boat.* I wanted that; I knew that much. We probably learn more about what we desire from seeing what we don't want than from seeing what we *do.* The lack of affection in my parents' marriage made me yearn to have a relationship in which I'd be hugged and kissed and looked at in "that way." I knew I didn't want any yelling. I knew I wanted to be happy. But the greatest lesson I took away from observing my parents was that I knew I wanted to have a marriage in which I could express my wants and needs.

I would argue that I had a better than average childhood with better than average parents. And despite their not seeming to support each other emotionally with complete success, they did support us—not perfectly, not entirely, but respectably. My parents were, like so many others are, I imagine, trying their best to do what they thought was right for their kids, sometimes hitting the mark and sometimes not. I grew up feeling confident, smart, happy, healthy, and loved, from my alphabet blocks to my college applications, just as my liberal, freethinking, ex-hippie parents had hoped I would. I also grew up thinking for myself, believing in my ideals, and questioning everything that was presented to me, regardless of the source or the subject—including sex, though I don't ever remember any real discussion of the topic. It was the late '70s and early '80s, and no one I knew had parents who talked to them much about sex. We were exposed to it everywhere, but somehow no one seemed to know a damn thing about it.

I grew up Jewish, and my father was a rabbi. I don't remember my dad or the synagogue ever telling me where Judaism stood on sexuality issues. I do, however, remember being part of a national youth group that organized several retreats each year. Various families from the hosting congregations would put us up in their homes, and I was always amazed that they would allow boys and girls to sleep in the same room together. Although plenty of making out went on, the group dynamic seemed to keep things fairly innocent. There weren't any orgies or drinking fests, nothing like the parties students from my high school held when their parents were out of town, which often resulted in the neighbors' calling the police. Interesting what happens when you give people—yes, even teenagers—freedom, instead of attempting to control their every move.

So I didn't get much in the way of sex ed. *The Joy of Sex* was on the shelf in our family room, and I remember leafing through its pages when I was ten or eleven and being perplexed by how the mechanics worked, and why anyone would do such things. The line drawings seemed so foreign and exotic. But the book's frank descriptions, and its placement next to other titles like *Captain in a Day: How to Sail Your Own Boat* or *Macramé the Easy Way: Ten Steps to Creating Perfect Plant Hangers,* made me believe that sex was just another leisure activity—nothing to be embarrassed about, nothing to hide.

The only sex talks I got from my parents came too late—like the one during Thanksgiving my freshman year of college. I brought my boyfriend home with me, and as we waited for the train that would take us back to school, my mother asked me to take a walk with her, a request that was generally not a good sign. I have never seen a volcano erupt, but the way the words gushed from my mother's lips—with a ferocity I have never seen before or since—must have been akin to what the witnesses of Vesuvius experienced.

"I don't know if you're having sex or if you've ever had sex or if you're planning on having sex and I know I'm not the person you would talk to about it even though I wish I was and I don't know if you're being careful if you know what I mean by being careful of course you know what I mean by being careful you better know what I mean by being careful but people die from sex now and when I was young you could get pregnant or need a shot of penicillin but not die and now you die but not always but you can and you're too young to have a baby and I want so much more for you and I know you want so much more for yourself and I don't know if you've had sex or are planning to have sex but I want you to be careful. . . . "

"I lost my virginity to Kevin last spring, and I went on the pill immediately," I finally interrupted. I was sure she would be very happy and proud.

"What?" she screeched. "Under my roof?" Thankfully, the train came not two minutes later, and she never, ever brought it up again.

The sex talk with my father happened that summer, when he picked me up from school to bring me back home.

"You're using condoms, right?" he said, apropos of absolutely nothing.

"Uh-huh," I answered.

"Good. So, do you want to catch an Orioles game tomorrow night?"

The only other conversation my mom and I had had was when I'd gotten my period, but she'd said little more than that it meant I was growing up, and that it was a happy thing that I shouldn't be scared of or embarrassed about. I have pitiful memories of trying to teach myself how to use a tampon, waddling through my aunt's house like a penguin because I didn't quite understand how the damn things were supposed to work. As for sex, my friends talked about "doing it," but none of my close friends seemed clear on just what "it" was until high school—where the mixed messages became even more baffling.

I went to a Catholic high school. It was the best private school in the area, and my dad taught Judaism classes for the Jewish students. The nuns and priests preached abstinence before marriage, and advocated antihomosexuality. I remember Father Keith coming into the classroom one day to talk to us about the AIDS epidemic. It was 1986. "The good thing is, you kids have nothing to worry about because, of course, you are not involved in any sort of . . . " (here he lowered his voice and looked at us sternly) " . . . sexual behavior. It's a gay disease, really; it's God's punishment for behavior that forsakes him and his great love for us."

I was sixteen years old, and one of my best friends, Theo, was gay. My parents had never had any problem with homosexuality. They raised us to believe that everyone is equal, regardless of age or race or sex, and certainly regardless of whom they love. I was both appalled and indifferent. Father Keith's comment struck me as awful, yet I wasn't affected by it, either, mostly because I chose to ignore what he was saying. I had enough brains and experience at that point to know that he was off base, and that I didn't agree with him, but not enough to take him on in front of my whole class.

Plenty of kids I knew were having sex in high school. And I wanted to. I didn't know why; it just seemed—like a lot of things—to be the thing to do. I just never had the opportunity. Although my best girlfriend, Janelle, was the head cheerleader and I could sit anywhere I wanted to in the cafeteria, I was never invited to any parties or asked out by any football players. The guys whom I imagined I would want to have sex with didn't even know I existed. I felt like I was waiting for the right person, right time, right something, but it wasn't quite clear what.

"You'll know," Janelle told me.

"How?"

"Trust me. You just will. You'll know he's really into you and won't fuck you over."

"That's what I'm looking for? Someone who won't fuck me over?"

"Well, that's not the only thing. You also want it to be someone you love and trust, and who loves and trusts you and all that. But you don't want to be the talk of the entire school the next day, do you?"

"I don't know. No," I managed, though it seemed as if I was the only girl at school who hadn't had sex yet.

"Yeah. Once you do it, that's fine. But you have to act like you haven't, and like you never would, because nice girls don't give it up until they're married."

"Oh," I said. I must have looked as confused as I sounded, because Janelle came over and started to French braid my hair—1984 girl-speak for *There, there, everything's going to be okay.*

"You have to be cool. That's all. It's cool to do it, but not for people to know. Except for the right people, and then they're not supposed to know everything—otherwise, it's not special." I was glad she was sitting behind me, because I could not have hidden the look on my face for all the money in the world. If I had looked perplexed before, I can't even imagine how mystified I must have seemed at that moment.

In a way, not much has changed for me this many years later. I feel equally baffled by contradictory signals and societal messages that make no sense whatsoever. Some things never change. But I did survive growing up, as most of us invariably do, despite all those puzzling notions about looks and love and sex and relationships. And, like so many other young girls, I thought I could and would eventually fall in love with a man who would fulfill every desire I'd ever had, and that I'd never want to be with anyone else. I thought we would live out the ideal I'd been raised to believe in. If people had told me back then that someday I'd be in an open marriage, and that I would be the one who had prompted it, I would have laughed in their faces. I had every irrational reason to believe, despite the fact that I was still a virgin, that my special someone—The One—was out there. All I had to do was wait, and someday my prince would come.

Chapter 2

my orgasm, my self

When she was seventeen, she lost her virginity to a guy who told her that she was responsible for her own orgasms. She set off for college feeling confident about her sexuality; she had several relationships and many lovers, and she was happy.

during my senior year of high school, I finally "knew," in exactly the way Janelle had told me I would, that I had found the guy I was prepared to lose my virginity to. Believe it or not, he was someone my mother set me up with—under the guise of helping me find a summer job.

"He's a counselor at a boys' camp, and his mother said the girls' camp is looking for someone to create a theater program for them. You'd be perfect for that!" my mom gushed. I knew right away that she was up to something. She said I would be "perfect" for something only when it had nothing to do with me, and everything in the world to do with her. I agreed to meet the guy just the same. It wasn't as if I was having any luck finding a boyfriend on my own.

A week later, I sat watching from my bedroom window as a young guy in a Chevy Nova pulled into our driveway. Even from that vantage point, I could tell he was cute, with his pretty-boy looks and rock-star hair. He was about five foot ten, with a prickly mustache and a face like Kiefer Sutherland's. He wore a fitted, lavender Izod with the collar flipped up, Guess jeans that were entirely too tight, and docksiders.

"Hey," he said when I opened the door for him. "Kevin." He put out his hand and I shook it.

"Hey," I replied.

"Hello, Debbie," he said to my mom, who was standing in the doorway that led from the kitchen to the foyer. She lifted her hand to wave but didn't say a word. She looked stunned. I didn't find out until after the date that she had never met Kevin, and that she'd built up a mental image of what she thought he'd look like—a quiet artist type, not some "gigolo wannabe," as she called him.

He took me to a Chinese restaurant in the mall and ordered a bottle of wine. He was so confident that the waiter didn't even hesitate. When Kevin saw the look of surprise on my face, he just winked and said, "It's cool."

Kevin was three years older than I was. When we met, he was about to turn twenty-one and I was about to turn eighteen. He was so sophisticated and mature, so slick. I was sure a guy like that would never be interested in the drama-club nerd I saw myself as back then. I was sure he would see in an instant that he was way too cool for me. I was in awe.

When the waiter returned to pour our wine and take our order, Kevin ordered for us. No one had ever ordered for me before, and I felt so grown-up. His gesture seemed romantic and adult—and cocky, which I liked. The only boys I'd gone out with had been fellow debate-team members who generally relied on me to call the shots. I felt like I'd won the teenage lottery.

"Is your real name Jennifer?" he asked after the waiter walked away.

"Uh-huh. Why?"

"Well, Jenny's such a little girl's name, and you are no little girl." He reached across the table and took my hand. "Is it okay if I call you Jennifer?"

"Uh-huh," I managed. I felt like I was on *Candid Camera,* as if any minute my dad was going to jump out from behind the fake palm, laughing as the camera crew revealed itself.

Back then, I was extremely insecure about how I looked and how guys saw me; I was always aware of not being on par with my classmates, many of whom looked like they could have given Brooke Shields a run for her money. At that moment, though, sitting across from Kevin, I finally saw a glimmer of hope. Here was this guy, this hunk, flirting with me, showing off for me. I felt my own power as I sat across from him that night, the power of my own sexuality and allure. And I liked it—a lot. I have heard people say that we're attracted to the people who reflect the vision of ourselves we most want to see, and I loved the sexy girl Kevin's baby blues were mirroring back to me that night.

The minute the bill came, he swiped it off the table. I reached for my purse.

"I got it, babe." No one had ever called me "babe" before, and again, I felt as if I were trapped in some sort of surreal world, as if this guy had swooped in out of nowhere to rescue me from teenage obscurity. I was overwhelmed by the feelings he awakened in me.

When he dropped me off at home, he opened my car door and walked me to my front door. "Call you tomorrow?" he asked. In that moment, I was convinced that it wouldn't be long before we slept together. He started calling me his girlfriend about a week later. In May, he took me to my senior prom and was every bit the perfect date. He made me feel pretty and smart and sexy and talented. He helped me to shed the dork cloak that I had been hiding under for so long. I wasn't even out of high school, so it wasn't as if I was thinking about getting married, per se, but he made me believe I was a catch, and I had, perhaps for the first time, that feeling that someday, someone would undoubtedly want to marry me.

My parents were ambivalent about my dating Kevin. But I was happy, and I wasn't drinking or using drugs or staying out too late, so they didn't have much to complain about.

It wasn't long after prom that I decided I was ready to sleep with him. It was as ideal a first time as I could have dreamed up. His parents were away, and he set up a romantic tableau, complete with candles and music. He had never pressured me; he had waited until I was ready. "I want you to be sure," he told me that night. "I don't want to be that asshole who 'took' your virginity."

"I'm sure," I said. "I love you."

"I love you too."

Afterward, I cried. Not about anything, really—almost as a release, I guess, or maybe even as a substitute for the orgasm I hadn't had, didn't know how to have.

"Oh god, are you okay? Are you sorry we did this?" he asked.

"No. No, no, no," I assured him. "I'm just . . . wow . . . I'm just . . . I can't believe I'm not a virgin anymore."

"So . . . it was okay?"

"Of course. It was great. I'm so glad it was with you."

"I am too," he said. "Want to do it again?"

"Uh-huh." The second time around, I willed myself to let go and allowed my body to take over. Kevin rolled onto his back, pulling me on top of him. At that moment, I understood what it meant for something to come naturally. I moved my body rhythmically with his, and came in a way that made my private fumblings in the dark seem like sparklers compared with these fireworks. I was hooked.

Later that night, Kevin turned to me and said the words that were to become the mantra of my sexuality: "You are responsible for your own orgasms." He told me that I had to ask for what I wanted and needed, and that there was nothing worse than expecting one's partner to be a mind reader. It was a new opening, and it forever shifted the way I looked at my own sexuality. Granted, because this was my first sexual experience, Kevin's comment set the bar quite high in terms of my owning what I wanted and getting what I needed, but there it was.

my breakup with Kevin was as hurtful

as our relationship had been wonderful. I found out from friends that he was sleeping with another girl while we were working at adjacent summer camps: a Swedish exchange student, of all people, named Olga. I felt stupid and rejected, ugly and small, when I finally laid eyes on her. She was his age and seemed so worldly. She was tall and blond—and had boobs. I totally understood why he'd want her instead of me.

After some weeks of dealing with my heartache, I finally crawled out of my teenage drama and begin to see the whole experience for what it was. I was lucky. My first time had been with a guy I loved and trusted, and who made me feel confident about my sexuality and my own reign over it. And even losing him to every boy's porn fantasy didn't negate that.

I felt alternately empowered by and terrified about my experiences with Kevin. On one hand, I felt cocky and secure ("I've been down love's rocky road, and I refuse to fall prey to its terrain"), and on the other hand, I felt terrified ("I'm never going down that road again. It's too painful"). But ultimately, I spent so many hours talking to Janelle about what dating in college would be like that Kevin started to seem inconsequential.

By the end of that summer, I was excited about the freedom that awaited me in college. I was glad that I had loved Kevin, but also happy that I'd built up a degree of callousness after having my heart broken. I decided I was going to protect myself and not be so quick to trust just anyone with my heart. Lesson learned: Love is not a guarantee of anything. And if you open yourself to enjoying it, you also open yourself to being crushed by it. Not that I wasn't still looking for love; I figured Tennyson must have known what he was talking about when he wrote, "Better to have loved and lost than never to have loved at all."

"It's good," Janelle told me. "You've had your firsts—first love, first fuck, first heartbreak—and now you can move on." Somehow, I knew she was right. Maybe it was because I'd read Judy Blume's young-adult novel *Forever* so many times, and had witnessed the protagonist, Kat, transition from losing her virginity to the boy she loved to falling for another guy, and perhaps it really was because of how amazing my first time had been. Or maybe it was just about trusting that this was how these things go. I had grown up hearing and believing that I would date lots of people before I found The One. So, even in the depths of my own drama, I knew I was at the beginning, rather than the end, of something big.

Part of my getting over Kevin also involved thinking a lot about the nature of monogamous relationships. We were young, true, but the whole time I had been faithful to and totally smitten by him, doing what I was "supposed" to do by being a committed girlfriend, he had been cheating on me. And he had just proceeded with our relationship as if nothing had changed between us. I had to stop and wonder for a moment just what his actions meant, and I was unable to reconcile my thoughts about the situation. Of course, Kevin's behavior spoke to his character, but it also made me realize that I would rather have known about his infidelity, and have been able to decide for myself where our relationship would go, than find out the way I did.

Still, it's nearly impossible for me to conceive of any other outcome than breaking up with Kevin. At eighteen, I wouldn't have dreamed of being in an open relationship, and

I cannot imagine that Kevin would have dared to ask that we try something like that, or that the concept would have crossed his mind. It certainly didn't cross mine. It didn't fit into any paradigm that existed in my eighteen-year-old consciousness. Kevin just figured he'd have his cake while, uh, eating the camp nurse's, too. But had he said, "I want to see other people," and had I been free to do the same, I have a feeling that it wouldn't have left such a sour taste in my mouth. So ultimately, just as Kevin opened some doors for me about taking control of my own sexuality, he also established the foundation of my thinking about the importance of openness and honesty in relationships, even when that honesty might be painful, which it almost always is.

it wasn't until years later that I started

to put these thoughts together for myself, and began to understand the roots of my own feelings about honesty and communication and just being open to, well, being open. But my early apprehension about the nature of monogamy, and just how problematic it can be, jumps out at me now in hindsight. When I read *Anatomy of Love,* by Helen Fisher, as an adult, I saw articulated exactly what was going on in my teenage head as I was getting ready for college: "Despite our cultural taboo against infidelity," Fisher writes, "Americans are adulterous. Our social mores, religious teachings, friends and relatives, urge us to invest all of our sexual energy on one person. . . . But in practice a sizable percentage of men and women spread their time, their vigor, and their love among multiple partners. . . . "[1]

When I look back on my first breakup, I realize (somewhat objectively, I think) that Kevin got things from both Olga and me. I needn't have been jealous, and his choice to be with her shouldn't have made me feel bad about myself. I was a person he was drawn to, and so was she. He should have been more honest with us, to be sure, but I now realize that he was searching for something that humans are biologically programmed to seek: variety. I realize now that he didn't have to love or want me any less in order to also want someone else—though we are certainly socialized to believe that this should not be the case.

Alfred C. Kinsey, the famed biologist whose research in the field of human sexuality shook the scientific world in 1948 with the publication of *Sexual Behavior in the Human Male* and *Sexual Behavior in the Human Female,* wrote, "Many females find it difficult to understand why any male who is happily married should want to have coitus with any female other than his wife."[2] And that's where I found myself. I would argue that most women whose husbands and boyfriends cheat on them find themselves incapable of believing that it's possible to be happily committed and cheating simultaneously. I didn't think Kevin was happy with both of us. My immediate reaction was one of self-criticism and doubt—that his wanting to be with Olga could mean only that he was unhappy being with me. But now I'm able to see how he could have wanted to have both of us for different reasons. It's just that both Olga and I wanted to be Kevin's one and only, as people generally want to be the sole focus of their partner's affections. But what if that desire were purely societal and we could rid ourselves of it? Jealousy thrives only when you feed it.

Jealousy is not a feeling generated by our biology; it's societally derived. Some people attest that jealousy keeps their relationships exciting, while for others it's a destructive force. Some people feel that a partner's jealousy is proof of the depth of the partner's feelings for them. I can certainly see how people create the idea of jealousy out of their fruitless need to own and fulfill completely another person's sexuality, and that jealousy only generates more jealousy. In their groundbreaking 1972 book *Open Marriage,* Nena and George O'Neill explain, "Jealousy is primarily a *learned* response, determined by cultural attitudes."[3] We foster jealousy in ourselves by thinking we own someone, and that we can be everything in the world for that person. Then we become unhappy when we find that we can't. The entire idea of being sexually exclusive and wholly possessing our spouses, the O'Neills point out, "breeds deep-rooted dependencies, infantile and childish emotions, and insecurities."[4] What if, instead, we were to feel secure in our relationships and acknowledge our needs and our partner's needs? We would have greater security and acceptance in our relationships, and we would nurture trust and honesty, instead of jealousy. As the saying goes, we reap what we sow.

In *The Myth of Monogamy,* David P. Barash and Judith Eve Lipton share the thoughts of a man living in Africa with two wives, who explains that although he is equally desirous of both of them, he is "wearied" by whichever one he is with after a few days with her. But then, he continues, "When I go to the other I find that I have greater passion; she seems more attractive than the first. But this is not really so, for when I return to the latter again there is the same renewed passion."[5]

I have no desire to be one of many wives, but I agree with this man's sentiment that having multiple partners invigorates our interest in each of them. Humans crave newness and variety, and having the same thing day in and day out becomes mundane. If I were to eat Italian food for several days in a row, for instance, I might want to go out for Chinese one night, which would only make the next Italian meal I ate more enjoyable. On a more profound level, experiencing other people, either sexually or otherwise, can similarly inform our other relationships.

I can understand not only how Kevin found pleasure with Olga, but also how his time with her made him appreciate his time with me more. Of course, lying and inequity were involved, and I wasn't afforded the same freedoms Kevin was granting himself. And that was ultimately the central issue for me. I wasn't mature enough at that age to wrap my head around the concept of an open relationship, but I do know that the idea of dating other people would have at least pushed the conversation in that direction. And had all three of us been in on the plan . . . who knows? But at that point, I simply had no model for a lifestyle like that. All I knew was monogamy—it was how nice girls did relationships. However, from my adult perspective as someone who's happy in her open marriage, I'm not surprised at all that Kevin was able to maintain our relationship so well—he was feeling happy and fulfilled all around, and that spilled over into our relationship dynamic. According to the O'Neills, "Outside sexual relationships, when they are in the context of a meaningful relationship, may be rewarding and beneficial to an open [relationship]."[6] If you are in a solid relationship in which you discuss openly what you're doing, other partners can actually improve your coupled life by providing the "otherness" that your original partner can't.

Bringing another person into the picture can make a static relationship less so. That's not to say it can make a disastrous relationship suddenly perfect, and it's not for everyone, to be sure; but you might be surprised by how easy the transition can be, especially if affairs have already, or have always, been part of your marital equation. Admittedly, I offer this advice in hindsight, as my initial reaction to Kevin's cheating on me involved none of this openness toward openness. At that point, I was just plain confused.

What had happened to my Ken, my Prince Charming? This wasn't how it was supposed to go. What had I done wrong? Surely I hadn't been enough for him; otherwise I would have been able to keep him all to myself.

heading off to college, I was armed

with four "truths" that I thought were vital to experiencing the new world I was entering: I could be whoever I wanted to be; I could experiment and learn; it was okay for sex to be fun and happy; and I would embrace it not only as good, but also as perfectly acceptable. With this attitude, I felt sure that I'd be able to fall in love, have my heart broken, and still survive. Having a healthy viewpoint about sex enabled me to get what I wanted out of the relationships I pursued without hurting the people I was with or getting hurt myself.

What I learned by approaching college from this perspective was that there were lots of options out there. When I arrived at school, I jumped headlong into exploring my newfound freedom. I made a conscious decision to follow my own feelings, rather than what other people told me I should feel about the unbreakable connection between sex and love. I didn't feel an urge to "go wild" or prove anything. Instead, I felt content and secure, confident in my sexuality and matured by my personal experience with relationships' impermanence. I had no idea what I was in for, of course—I still managed to get my heart broken and go after guys who weren't interested in me—but I also felt as prepared as a girl could possibly be, thinking for myself, owning my sexuality, and accepting that the best I could do was give it a whirl.

I vividly remember my first day of college. "This is going to be so great," I said to Ellen, my new roommate. "Zillions of guys on this campus, and no one to tell us when to come home!"

Her apprehensive look surprised me.

"You don't mean sleeping with them, do you?" she asked.

I suddenly felt very uncomfortable. It was immediately clear to me that she and I had vastly different ideas about sex. "Yeah, actually, that kind of *is* what I meant," I said. "Not with all of them, of course. Just a few." I hoped my attempt at a joke would help, but despite her nervous giggle in response to my quip, I could feel the anxiety rising in her.

"I . . . I . . . I don't believe you should have sex before marriage, that's all."

"Oh." I didn't know quite what to do with this information, but it was obvious that we might not make the best roommates.

"So, you're a virgin," I said.

Ellen nodded.

"That's cool. More for me, then." I swatted her with a pillow. I would have done nearly anything to break the tension and end that conversation. I didn't think that moment was the best opportunity to tell her my thoughts on love and sex. I wanted to tell her about my first time, about what Kevin had taught me, and about how we owed it to ourselves to own our sexuality. Now was our time; this was our chance to check it all out before we settled down. And I did truly believe that I was going to settle down, find the right guy and all the rest. But I also knew that I had some oat sowing to do, and that there was nothing wrong with that. I felt confident that my college years would be my sexual experimentation years, when I would find The One by testing out various scenarios and partners and discovering which of my trial runs I might want to become my lifelong reality. How ironic that being open is supposed to prepare us for a lifetime of being closed.

Throughout college, I had this sense that I was shopping for Mr. Right by trying on many Mr. Maybes. It was the late '80s and early '90s, and life for young women my age centered on dating, which focused on finding someone to marry. And most of us made sure to have our fun while it lasted. We felt distinctly that these were the best years of our lives; we talked about what settling down was going to be like, and a lot of us felt confused and conflicted. If we were enjoying our freedom so much now, was it really possible that our lives were going to be even better in the future, as we were told they would?

Even as we continued to question this notion's validity, we still somehow believed that everything would unfold naturally—that security, well-being, and someone who would "complete" us were waiting just around the corner. In a very

Ozzie and Harriet sort of way, I was bizarrely focused on the classic mores of finding someone to spend my life with, yet simultaneously enjoying dating lots of people, and finding it the most sexually liberating experience I'd ever had. By day, I was marching on Washington, lobbying at the General Assembly, and taking classes in women's studies; by night, I was making dinner and playing housewife for whichever boyfriend I had at the time. And though this way of being conflicted with my desires for freedom and individuality, no other behavior occurred to me. I was conditioned to believe in acting a certain way with my boyfriends, and not until years later did I realize that that behavioral mode was not my only option.

my first college boyfriend, Travis, was

a guy I met in my honors English class. He was an intellectual. We'd stay up late into the night, smoking Camels and arguing about abortion rights and feminism and Dante. We had great sex. We talked dirty and tried things I'd never done before. He helped me build even further upon the security about my own sexual habits and curiosity, and the acceptance of others' sexual habits, that I had begun developing in my relationship with Kevin. He admired my attitude about sex and wasn't put off by my ownership of my sexuality. We never talked specifically about monogamy, but I know that neither of us slept with anyone else while we were together. I didn't need or want anything or anyone else, and when we broke up six months later, it was mutual.

I learned a lot from Travis. He made me take myself seriously as a person, as an academic, and as a sexual being. Because of my deep connection with him, the next couple of guys I dated were barely blips on my radar. I had a few other boyfriends, relationships that would last a few months and then die away. Despite the brevity of those connections— or perhaps because of it—an agreement always existed (sometimes discussed, sometimes simply understood) that we wouldn't see other people. When I was involved with a man, I automatically expected that he would be my guy and I'd be his girl. It never felt like a sacrifice or a compromise, though, because these relationships ultimately weren't serious commitments. And because they were not particularly serious, the issue of cheating simply never arose. People cheat because they want to continue their current relationship (whether for love or convenience or otherwise) while indulging their desire. If that were not the case, people would simply leave their primary relationship rather than cheat. Since I wasn't involved in relationships that either my partners or I were deeply invested in, we simply broke up, as opposed to seeing other people on the sly. Outside of marriage, it's normal and possible and expected to date this way as long as both parties concur. Within a marriage, though, the options are much more limited if you want to see other people: Either you're open or you're committing adultery.

Back then, I didn't even consider that so many marriages might be adulterous. I didn't personally know couples who were cheating, because I was still a kid. I simply accepted at face value the party line I was being fed at every turn, about finding the perfect man and riding off into the sunset with him toward a lifetime of wedded bliss.

Outside of the more committed relationships I was pursuing, I did have a few experiences that taught me about the type of freedom I craved in sexual relationships. Having partnerships in which the parameters of both parties' expectations were clear from the get-go, with no question about what each person wanted, made for very fulfilling sex, regardless of emotional connection. In a September 2007 article for *Glamour* magazine entitled "10 Sex Questions Every Woman Should Ask Herself," author Hilda Hutcherson, an ob-gyn in New York City and a clinical professor at Columbia University, writes, "Sex is always better and more deeply satisfying when your motivation for doing it is simple and healthy."[7] One great reason to have sex that Hutcherson lists is: "You're horny, pure and simple." By the time I got to college, I believed that sex for sex's sake was okay. And as much as this idea felt good and right to me, I now think, in retrospect, that I was also hoping subconsciously that these feelings would just go away, because I didn't want to confront what those beliefs could ultimately mean—that I might never be satisfied in a monogamous relationship.

The message I got growing up had been that sex is only good when it happens in a relationship between two people who love each other. But what I discovered instead was that love, sex, and relationships—or any combination thereof—could be good or happy or successful when the participants' expectations were shared and understood. What marked the difference between sex in a relationship and a singular sexual experience were time and commitment. Otherwise, the sex could be remarkably, similarly satisfying. I enjoyed the range of experiences I had—the committed and the noncommitted ones. I was exploring as opportunities presented themselves, partaking in the ones that suited me and bowing out of others. I was exercising my ability to choose, a right I had been raised to appreciate and claim.

Finally, my junior year, I did meet a guy who seemed like the type of person I could settle down with and marry. My parents had never told me specifically that I had to settle down with a nice guy someday, but all cultural signs sure seemed to be pointing me in that direction. The messages were all around and constantly whispering in my ear: *Meet a guy, capture his attention, fall in love, get him to propose, and marry him.* As E. J. Graff writes in her book *What Is Marriage For?* "Trained from birth to ask ourselves what we want to be when we grow up, how can Americans be expected to guide our marital and sexual hopes and lives by anything but that same inner voice?"[8]

My own inner voice was practically drilling a hole through my skull by the time I met Clark. Something about him made me feel like he could be *that* guy. He was steady and mature, and he seemed to embody everything I was supposed to want in a man. He looked like a Ken doll—handsome and preppy in his Ralph Lauren sweater and Weejun loafers. I certainly didn't see it then, but I sure do recognize it now: He was my Ken doll and I was his Barbie. I'm sure I looked the same to him as he did to me—like someone who could fit into this whole "real life" thing. I had to pick someone eventually, right? So why not him? Despite all of that "trust your own experience" stuff my parents had raised me on, and the four "truths" I thought I was following to a tee, the real truth was that I was completely blinded by social conditioning. Its voice was crystal clear, and it was saying, *Pick one already.*

Clark made me feel as if I *wanted* to be his Barbie, too—the "perfect" girl to his "perfect" guy. He likened himself to the architect character, Michael Steadman, and me to the loyal housewife, Hope, from the TV show *thirtysomething,* and we both took to our roles frighteningly easily.

Susan Faludi writes about *thirtysomething's* antifeminism in her famous manifesto, *Backlash.* Of one of the show's numerous scenes that depicts Hope in her happy-homemaker persona, Faludi writes, "The good mother . . . was bathed in heavenly light as she floated about the kitchen, rapturous over breastfeeding."[9] The irony of it all was not lost on me. I wasn't missing the show's overarching message. Quite the contrary—not only was I fully aware of it, but I was also becoming more and more aware of the plethora of contradictions within which we must inevitably live if we are to follow the social mores of our day. I knew of the perils of the roles, and yet I stepped in headlong just the same. Like a wearied follower of Jim Jones, I felt compelled to drink the Kool-Aid. The human brain can withstand only so much of even the most obvious and counterintuitive brainwashing.

Faludi continues, "Meanwhile, the bad spinsters clutched their barren wombs and circuited miserably around the happy Steadman household."[10] Even the image the family's last name invokes—that of a steady man—was chosen to imply the safety and security that any woman should want. And that was what I was seeking, along with every other woman I knew.

When I broke up with Clark years later, the last thing he said to me was, "If you see Hope, tell her I miss her." It was creepy, but the turns my relationship with Clark took proved important in my long, meandering journey toward understanding what would ultimately make me happy in a partnership. After we had dated for a few years (classic boyfriend/girlfriend stuff, with lots of going out and plenty of sleeping over at each other's apartment without ever living together), Clark headed off to architecture school in another state. After he had been away for a few months, I told him that I wanted the freedom to see other people, and he obliged.

I dated a few guys. Mostly, though, I just had flings: some one-night stands and a couple more sustained relationships—friendships with benefits, I suppose. It wasn't that I was really looking for someone else to love. I loved Clark. But I saw him only once a month and I missed having sex. Looking back, I realize that was really my first stab at the open-relationship thing. It wasn't exactly "cheating" (I had his permission and all), but it certainly did not have the hallmarks of a healthy open relationship—the honesty and communication. It was more of a "don't ask, don't tell" thing, and because of that, I never felt 100 percent okay about it. Since Clark didn't want to discuss our arrangement, I couldn't help but wonder whether he was truly comfortable with it.

For a while, I balanced my relationship with Clark with my outside flings. I still felt like I wanted—or at least should want—to be with Clark and have a more traditional relationship, because that's what I expected of myself, for myself. Little did I know then how young our American idea of a "traditional" relationship actually is. As it turns out, Graff reports, "the nuclear family has so recently become the standard household unit that U.S. demographers can't accurately track it before 1940."[11] Amazing how a convention so young can rule an entire society with such unrelenting force.

What came before that? Simply put, anything and everything: extended families; families with a plethora of stepchildren; children placed in the homes of their future in-laws; boarders, lodgers, servants, and anyone else living under one roof; children living in homes where they were more employees than kids; children of the wealthy living with wet nurses or other caretakers.[12] Depending on their wealth, status, and trade, couples and families lived in any number of permutations that might be called families, because "families" meant people who lived together. The definition had nothing—nothing—to do with love. Children then were not considered as precious as they are now. Economics dictated marriage and living arrangements. Nothing more and nothing less. Therefore, to stress the importance and history of a man and a woman's falling in love and living together and having children they dote on is nothing short of newfangled. Yet the idea of the nuclear family as the cornerstone of human existence seems to be common knowledge.

I was lucky, I believe, to have had this early opportunity to have an open, albeit not ideal, relationship. It allowed me to sample different experiences while still having the steady and secure relationship I craved. I knew I wanted both; I just didn't know then that I could *have* both. One night, when Clark was away, I decided to test something out. I had heard male friends talking about how they wished girls could just enjoy sex and not be all hung up about whether the guy would call the next day, or whether going home with someone meant a girl was a slut. The guys also said they probably couldn't trust a girl to actually do what they wished she would, because it would probably mean she had ulterior motives, like wanting to trick them into a relationship or accuse them later of treating her like a whore.

I had long noticed that I thought about sex differently than a lot of my close girlfriends did; my attitudes about it seemed more closely aligned with those of my guy friends. And because of where I was in my relationship with Clark, when I heard those guys talking, I figured my chance was now or never—I wanted to see what it would feel like to really sit in the driver's seat, to approach sex with what most people might define as a male sensibility.

And so, at a dinner party at my friend Cecile's house, when I found myself sitting across from a very cute guy, it suddenly occurred to me to do something most women weren't supposed to do. We had talked and flirted all evening, and it seemed obvious to me where things could go if one of us were to make a move.

I mouthed across the table to him, "Let's go back to my place."

"What?" he mouthed back.

"Christian and I are going out to buy some chocolate," I announced to our mutual friends at the table. "I cannot drink coffee without chocolate."

"You are a true pain in the ass," Cecile said.

"Thank you very much," I said to her. "Let's go," I said, looking back at him.

As soon as we got in the car, he turned to me and said, "Chocolate?"

"No," I replied. "Sex."

"Excuse me?" he said, gasping more than speaking.

"Chocolate I can do without right now, but sex with you I cannot. I thought we'd go by my house, get to it, and head back to the party. They're so drunk, they won't even miss us."

"But . . . "

"I know you live in California. I know you're not looking for a girlfriend. I know you're a nice guy, and you respect that I'm a nice girl. Blah, blah, blah. Look, some girls just want to get laid, too. It's sex, not rocket science."

We got back to Cecile's two fun, satisfying hours later. We pulled up to the side of the house and I parked the car.

"You're amazing," he said as he unbuckled his seat belt.

"What do you mean?" I asked.

"I had such a good time. And it seems like you had such a good time, too."

"I did."

"And neither of us is the worse for wear."

"Exactly," I said, feeling pleased. "It's just sex."

I never heard from Christian again. I didn't expect to. But I will never forget how that night made me feel. Sexy—not contrived sexy, but actually sexy. Sexy in the realm of things that tap into the most basic human desire: the small of a woman's back, the breadth of a man's shoulders, moistened lips, warm skin, curves and muscles, and the sensation of one body against another. All of those things are about flesh, not minds. Yes, being in love is sexy. Intelligence, humor, all of that can be very sexy. But at the end of the day, sun-freckled skin, strong limbs, warm breath—that's what we respond to sexually. And not just one of those things, but all of them or some of them or different ones at different times. Human nature dictates that the sexiest things are the ones that are new or different or surprising.

i have always enjoyed sex both within

a relationship and outside of one. I enjoy sex coupled with love, as well as sex without it. I enjoy different people at different times for different reasons. That interest is simply part of our biological makeup. In *The Myth of Monogamy,* Barash and Lipton write, "There is simply no question whether sexual desire for multiple partners is 'natural.' It is . . . [and] multiple mating doesn't refer only to the well-known tendency of males to seek numerous sexual partners, but to females too."[13]

And if that's how we're wired, then so be it. Monogamy might feel right for some people, might be necessary for others, but it's impossible to make a compelling argument for monogamy as "natural." According to Barash and Lipton, "In attempting to maintain a social and sexual bond consisting exclusively of one man and one woman, aspiring monogamists are going against some of the deep-seated evolutionary inclinations with which biology has endowed most creatures, *Homo sapiens* included."[14] I can think of few other instances—other than perhaps creationists, who insist on debunking evolutionary theory—in which such clear scientific evidence is so summarily dismissed.

The question for those of us who find this argument compelling is how to reconcile it. It's strange, really, because we do live in a culture of cheating. It's accepted, even taken for granted. We see it played out in literature *(Madame Bovary)* and film *(Match Point),* as well as in politics (Bill Clinton) and pop culture (Hugh Grant). "Adultery was an accepted everyday kinda thing in the southern Christian culture I grew up in. Common for a man to have a mistress for a lifetime and a wife," bell hooks writes in the 1999 *Ms.* magazine "adultery issue."[15]

The prevalence and general societal acceptance of cheating strike me as ironic because of how much flak I get for being in an open relationship. Though there's chatter about Clinton being a sex addict, or Grant being at it again, it doesn't affect these men's careers, or even seem to have caused them any particular angst. But imagine what would happen if the Clintons were to come forward and publicly announce that they're in an open relationship. God knows Hillary would neither be a U.S. senator nor be considered a viable presidential candidate. She would be seen as a pariah. But standing by her man when he cheated on her was what actually made people sympathetic to her and allowed them to see her as more human and flawed, just like the rest of us. Ironic, indeed.

And so, though the rates of adultery and divorce and marital dissatisfaction soar, open marriage is still considered beyond taboo—it's socially offensive. Society as a whole still clings to its ideals of heterosexual, monogamous relationships and, ultimately, marriage, while tacitly accepting cheating across the board. It's amazing to consider the hypocrisy of it all.

How can we accept cheating while holding monogamy up as the ultimate goal of long-term relationships? My theory is that we're so invested in the idea of monogamous relationships and marriages that the only way we have found to accommodate our nonmonogamous biology is to cheat. Fisher writes, "[A]lthough infidelity is commonplace among adults—and known to most because of the lack of privacy—a code of absolute silence prevails. Family life must not be undermined."[16] Our entire nation is practicing a "don't ask, don't tell" policy when it comes to philandering, yet it's a fragile arrangement that, more and more, is coming apart at the seams. It's a fine line to walk: Start exposing people, and you too might be exposed. Act like it's no big deal, and people might think you're one of "them."

I think we act the way we do because we are insecure in our own beliefs about how relationships should work, and we don't want to deal with the conflict we face when we stop to consider how they actually *do* work. We don't want to be judged for doing it wrong, so we participate in a classic form of distraction: finger pointing. "Look at how screwed up they are!" "Did you hear so-and-so is cheating?" But crying "cheater" only keeps us from acknowledging our own desires, or makes us think we won't be judged ourselves. The sad part is that in hiding, we perpetuate the myth about what marriages really do look like. No one wants to be the first to come out with the truth, but imagine how things could be if everyone decided to take that leap all at once.

Love and sex and relationships are a mushy concept as it is. And, like a handful of mud, if you cling to it too tightly, squeeze it desperately to hold on to it, it's guaranteed to ooze messily through your fingers in the form of exposed affairs, broken hearts, shattered marriages, and wrecked families. The truth is this: We want it all. We want to be able to seek out other relationships, sexual and otherwise, but we don't want to lose our committed relationships, because we gain enjoyment, security, and privilege from them. And so people cheat and work out their relationships in the aftermath of exposure, or they don't. Either way, they too often avoid, at almost all costs, being honest about their needs and desires.

There are all sorts of reasons why our society doesn't accept open marriage as a viable solution. Jealousy is high on that list. We have an often overwhelming desire to be someone's one and only, even if and when we don't reciprocate. Our biology and our behavior actually support the structure open marriage offers, but our brains refuse to follow. "Monogamy's not ideal for everyone and shouldn't be promoted as the ideal or default relationship setting," Liza, a woman I interviewed online, told me. Liza is twenty years old and in an open relationship with a married man. "I think people cheat because they get bored or they feel attracted to someone else, both of which are inevitable and can't be prevented," she continues.

For others, cheating is about excitement and adventure—it's only fun because it's not allowed. But for many people, it's the only means of finding fulfillment without risking the security of their current relationships. I've personally never cheated for the thrill; I don't like it. It makes me nervous and paranoid, and it's difficult for me to enjoy something that I know has the potential to hurt, or is already hurting, someone else. And yet I eventually did cheat on my husband, an experience that, though very painful, helped me solidify my feeling that lying and betrayal are much worse than the act of having sex with another person.

I think it's because people want the freedom to cheat that they accept others' cheating. At the same time, we jump at the chance to publicly chastise anyone caught cheating, because we don't want others to think we're okay with it. Still, it looks to me like a lot of people *do* accept cheating, And as long as everyone's cool with turning a blind eye, everything is copasetic. Writes Kipnis, "It's not precisely adultery that's prohibited (after all, politicians have been doing it for centuries and everyone knows it), it's public acknowledgment that the system [marriage] needs propping up with these secret forms of enjoyment."[17]

This situation is not dissimilar from the fable "The Emperor's New Clothes." We walk around, pretending like everything's okay, because we don't want to call attention to this glaringly obvious thing that so many people are doing. We're collectively engaged in promoting the practice of cheating because we are too scared of more viable, healthy, and honest alternatives. Wouldn't it be better to live in a society based on honest open marriages, rather than deceptive traditional ones? I am well aware that some people will be waiting in the wings to declare how preposterous this suggestion is. For all of our talk about the importance of telling the truth and living honestly, hypocrisy in our society is more commonplace than dealing with the consequences of telling the truth. For me, the bottom line is clear: It's only cheating if it demands secrecy. Otherwise, it's simply being open.

Of course, for as closed as we seem to be, we do idolize some people who have embraced an open lifestyle wholly. Take Hugh Hefner, for example, and his lifetime of open relationships. He and his three girlfriends even have a wildly popular reality television show, *The Girls Next Door,* which chronicles life at the Playboy mansion. Rashes of people live vicariously through Hefner. Even more live secretly and or deceptively like him. But people still proclaim to be ardently opposed to that kind of lifestyle.

I'm not necessarily making a case for Hefner's particular style of open relationship. Kendra, at twenty-two, seems awfully young and naive. But Holly and Bridget, who are twenty-eight and thirty-four, respectively, seem well aware of the choice they have made, as well as what that choice means for them and how others may perceive it. Of course, despite their protests to the contrary, it is hard to believe that the perks (the money, the fame, the "opportunities") do not play a large part in their choice to be involved with Hefner. But aren't there all kinds of relationships in which such benefits factor into our decision to be with someone? How many people wouldn't like to "marry up"? And have you ever heard a woman say, "He doesn't have a job or any interest in working, but who cares"? Please. And if you watch enough episodes of *The Girls Next Door*, it's clear that there are some genuine feelings between Hefner and his girls. Regardless, they're making a personal choice, and they're living openly in a relationship that, at least for now and despite anyone else's reservations, is working for them. "With open relationships, people don't have to be repressed, and the people in the relationship don't have to disrespect one another by lying," Liza opines. Exactly. It's the difference between lying to ourselves and being honest about who we are and what the relationships we're in are like.

my own early dalliances in openness

eventually ended. Clark and I broke up. Some of my girlfriends held an intervention and told me that my wanting
to be with other guys could mean only one thing—that I
didn't really want to be with Clark. I didn't wholly concur
with their opinion, but I did listen to them. How could I not
have? How could they and the television and the movies
and the books and everything I'd been hearing my whole
life be wrong? I needed everyone else to be okay with my
choices, and I felt certain that if my friends saw a problem,
there must be something wrong with me and what I was
doing. So I broke up with him, crushing his heart and my
own. And, when it comes right down to it, I did it because I
wanted to sleep with other people.

After the breakup, I felt completely lost and wondered
what on earth I was going to do, and who on earth I would
date. The relationship left me questioning what I wanted.
Did I want to marry a Mr. Straight-and-Narrow? Did I not
want to get married at all, but instead buck the trend and
have a string of lovers? I was already starting to contemplate
the picture of what an open relationship might entail, but I
didn't know how to make it happen. I didn't know how to
find someone who would be receptive to the idea, and I
didn't know how to ask for what I wanted. Truth be told, I
wasn't even sure such a thing was possible outside of having
some sort of "fringe" lifestyle, which I definitely wasn't
interested in. All I knew was that I had always been looking

for something, and that that something didn't fit the mold of what other people wanted for me. But, for the first time in my life, I was starting to question what *I* really wanted.

Pursuing the answer to that question, I made my first foray into "girl world." I had never given much thought to dating or sleeping with women, but I was never actively opposed to it, either. I'd just never found myself in a position to explore—that is, until I met Sophie Anne. Shortly after Clark and I broke up, I went on tour as an actress with a children's theater company, and she and I instantly became the best of friends. How we also became lovers after that was a natural unfolding that felt like the craziest, but also the most logical, thing ever. It still feels that way even now, actually, more than ten years later.

I admitted to Sophie Anne that I had started to wonder what it would be like to kiss her. To my surprise and relief, she told me that she had wondered the same thing. My feelings that day, which are still vivid in my memory, were echoed recently in an article I read by Jennifer Baumgardner, author of *Look Both Ways,* in which she describes her first experience kissing a girl: "Then, because I couldn't stand not to, I kissed her."[18] My sentiments exactly. At that moment, it wasn't about what I should do, or even wanted to do. It was what I *had* to do, so I did it.

Sophie Anne and I began sleeping together and dated for about six months. We were never "out," however. We told a few close friends, but we were never girlfriends. Still, being together somehow felt sensible. We loved each other already. We were attracted to each other. We weren't hung up on sexual orientation. We just did what felt good to us for as long as it felt right. And when we were both ready to go back to being just friends, we did so fairly seamlessly.

Being with Sophie Anne was another step, another piece in the puzzle I was trying to solve, in my ongoing exploration of love, sex, and relationships. It was my first time with a woman, and it was short term and closeted at that. So I didn't know if I had simply fallen in love with her specifically, or whether I might be bisexual. If the latter was true, the idea of being in a working monogamous relationship seemed even more improbable than it already felt. How could I reconcile bisexuality with such an arrangement? Could I fall in love with just one person of either sex and give up the things that attracted me to the other sex? Did gender matter? Maybe I was looking for Cinderella, not Prince Charming—or maybe I was looking for them both.

Regardless of my experiences and feelings, I still felt the weight of the world on my shoulders, demanding that I get it all sorted out—and soon. I wasn't getting any younger, my grandmother was fond of reminding me. Anne Kingston, in her book *The Meaning of Wife,* boils down the social mandate women face to this: "Compromise, settle, tone yourself down, and do it sooner than later."[19] Those aren't anyone's exact words, of course, but they articulate the message I felt pressing down on me at every turn. It was time to figure out what I wanted.

Chapter 3
just pick
someone already

Then she met a nice guy whom she thought she could love. He was what she imagined she had always wanted— someone kind and smart, who would love her and take care of her. The summer they started dating, she slept with another woman, but then decided she was ready to settle down. He said "I do" and she said "I do," and for a while they were happy. Then they had a baby and their sex life plummeted, and she soon realized that her sex drive was far greater than his. And so she had an affair. She told him about it, and they decided they'd work on their marriage. After all, what else was there to do?

when I met Christopher, I was ready

for him. I felt like I had done all of my proverbial oat sowing, and I thought I was prepared to pick one person and get married. I figured I would be fine with it, happy, as long as I managed to choose that magical "right person." It was what everyone else did, and I was determined to succeed. What I was actually experiencing was the social pressure to get married that so many women fall prey to, and that they follow with such blind faith, that they eventually begin mistaking it for their own desire. I mean, what was so special about me that I should end up doing anything other than exactly what everyone else was doing?

I was ready to be with someone who saw me as more than a toy, someone who loved and respected and maybe even cherished me. Surely I wasn't going to find that in some casual relationship, and certainly not in a series of casual relationships, right? So when I met Christopher, it felt like the stars were aligning. He was *that guy.*

As it turned out, I had plans with another guy the day we met. I was all dressed up and ready to go out. I stood waiting, waiting, waiting for him to pick me up, but he never came. I decided that was it; I wasn't going to miss the festival we'd planned on going to just because some creep had stood me up, and I wasn't going to miss out on life because I was dating creeps. So I grabbed my bag and headed out the door.

As I walked down the street, I kept an eye out for people I knew. It wasn't a big city, and I was sure I'd run into someone. I reached into my bag to grab my lighter, to light the cigarette that was already dangling between my fingers, when I remembered the exact spot on my coffee table where I'd left it.

"Damn," I said, louder than I'd intended.

"Excuse me?" A tall, thin man was leaning against a nearby lamppost, surrounded by a group of guys I assumed to be his friends. They were drinking and laughing.

"I'm sorry. I just need a light, and I couldn't find my . . ." He held out a flame before I could even finish my sentence.

"Madame," he said.

"Thanks." I took a long drag and continued on my way.

"Wait a minute," he called after me, lifting his sunglasses to rest on his forehead. "You go to law school, right?"

"Uh, yeah. How do you know?"

"And you go to Cook's Corner almost every day for lunch with your crew."

"My crew?"

"You know, your group of brainiacs. Right?"

I nodded, unsure of exactly where this might be going.

"Hello, I'm Tom and I'll be your server."

"Oh my god," I said with a smile. I hadn't recognized him without his uniform of khaki pants and a blue oxford shirt; he looked so laid-back in his T-shirt and jeans. Tom introduced me to his friends, who insisted I join them when

I told them how I'd been stood up. One of those friends was Christopher, my now husband. I liked him straightaway. Tall, blond, great smile, broad shoulders. Smart as hell, with an incredibly dry wit. We hit it off immediately and made plans to see each other again a few nights later.

After our first date, we set another and then another. We had a good time together in bed. He was sweet and attentive. He seemed to like that I could be aggressive, but he was also happy to take the lead himself. It was satisfying, happy sex, no more and no less. It felt good, and like exactly what I wanted at the time. I had no desire to be ravaged by the big bad wolf. I thought that maybe I didn't need newness or excitement or pushing the envelope because—could it be?—I was falling in love.

Three months after we met, I had to go away for work for the whole summer, as a dancer in an outdoor theater production at the beach in Manteo, North Carolina.

"I'll come visit you," he said, standing at my car door, both of us tearing up. "Don't cry, okay? I'll call you. You'll be back before you know it." He leaned down and kissed me goodbye.

that summer was a lot of fun. It was

a wild place. Many of the dancers and actors had been performing in the show for years, and they had all sorts of rituals and parties. They also had a motto: "Come engaged, go home gay." Apparently, more than a few people dabbled in same-sex experimentation while there, and it did feel more like a commune than any summer-stock theater company I had ever experienced.

We spent our days at the beach, and our nights doing the show and then drinking and partying until way too late. The place was humming with sexual energy. Although Christopher and I hadn't said we would be exclusive, we had been since the day we met. So when Pierce, a fellow dancer, walked me back to my apartment one night after a party, I didn't kiss him when he leaned his body toward mine. I didn't even want to.

"I have a boyfriend," I told him.

"Really? That's the first time I've heard you say that," Pierce said.

It was true. I hadn't mentioned Christopher on purpose. I was enjoying all the attention and the flirting. It was exciting to be desired by other people who weren't my boyfriend. It was validating, too. I suppose we shouldn't need other people's attraction to us to prove our attractiveness or, worse, our worth. But even when we are fully aware of that fact, it can be difficult to separate ourselves from it—and so, for better or for worse, it felt damn good to be noticed.

Attraction is a natural drug. In her book *Anatomy of Love,* Helen Fisher explains a theory put forth by psychologist Michael Liebowitz that supposes that "the euphoria and energy of attraction are caused by a brain bath of naturally occurring amphetamines that pool in the emotional centers of the brain."[1] And boy, was I feeling the effects. Being desired felt amazing—it was a natural high, not unlike the one runners describe achieving from the increased endorphins that kick in when they run. My need was biological; my hesitation to indulge, merely societal. Only a week later, I decided to change my tune.

One woman there, Leila, had been more than suggestive with me since the very first day of the summer season. She'd come on to me in the most shocking way, whispering in my ear, just moments after we met, that she was going to fuck me by the end of the summer. At the time, I had thought she was drunk. "I wasn't drunk," she told me later. "I wanted you—and I get what I want." I couldn't argue with her on that point, because three weeks into our stay, I was naked in her bed following a night of sex—with her boyfriend watching. The two of us shattered all of poor Tim's boyhood ménage à trois dreams, and he expressed his disappointment when he found out that this particular threesome experience was about Leila's and my finding pleasure with each other, and that it had little to nothing to do with him.

When I walked into their bedroom earlier that night, I found Tim tied to the bed and her straddling him, pouring hot candle wax onto his naked chest. *This girl is nuts,* I thought. But I was also insanely turned on. My sex life with Christopher had been good, yes, but it had already become a bit predictable, even that early on. And now here was this woman: gorgeous body, insatiable drive, and an attitude about sex that I remembered having had myself, pre-Christopher. She reminded me of the me I was seriously contemplating giving up. She also made me remember how voracious a woman's sexual appetite can be. Her desiring me made my own longings seem all the more normal—and she was so unapologetic. I wanted her, without question, and I gave in more than willingly.

At that moment, I didn't care what the consequences might be as far as Christopher was concerned. The next morning, of course, I did. But I reminded myself that Christopher and I had been together only a few months, and that we had never even addressed monogamy or exclusivity. For all I knew, he was sleeping with someone else, too—at least that's what I told myself. Truth was, I felt like Leila would be the last girl I would ever be with—and I didn't want to pass up the opportunity. Even then, I was thinking Christopher would be the man I'd marry someday. Justification? Perhaps. But it was one amazing night.

In Leila's room, I could feel myself getting wet at the sound of her voice.

"Take your clothes off," she commanded. "All of them. Now." I obeyed, and every inch of my body suddenly remembered how much it liked something more than what Christopher and I had going on. As I undressed, Leila untied Tim and ordered him to stand at the side of the bed. She tied me down, straddled me, and dripped the wax from the candle she'd been using on Tim onto my skin, leaving thick, waxy trails down the length of my torso and across my breasts.

"It hurts," I said, pulling against the restraints.

"You don't think that's going to make me stop, do you?" she countered.

"No," I said. And I didn't want her to stop.

"Good girl," she said, removing the restraints and kissing me. Tim watched silently while we had sex. He knew better than to join in without Leila's invitation. She was in charge. When I heard him sigh, I looked up, expecting to see that he'd come. Instead I saw his disappointment, maybe mixed with a bit of fear.

"You girls don't need me at all, do you?" he said.

"No," Leila replied bluntly. "Want, maybe, but definitely not need."

"I'm gonna go," he said, pulling on his jeans and black Aerosmith T-shirt.

"Suit yourself," she said, without missing a beat.

I slept with Leila several times that summer. I also slept with Christopher when he came to visit me. She was manipulative and exhausting. He was sweet and smart and loving. By the end of the summer, I knew I wanted to spend the rest of my life with Christopher. Leila and I had had fun together, but I was ready to swear off being tied down with velvet ropes, splayed at someone else's mercy. I was twenty-five years old, and it was time to move on to a serious, committed relationship. It was time to be a grownup and settle down. All of this experimenting and sleeping around was kid stuff, I told myself. It had nothing to do with who I was. It was a phase. And it was over.

one year after Christopher and I met,

we were engaged, and one year after that, we were married. We lived in a rented condo for the first year, and then bought a cute little brick house in a fashionable part of town. I took to the role of wife quite naturally. I baked bread and kept a garden. I wore Lilly Pulitzer dresses and went to scrapbooking parties. Christopher and I had sex occasionally, far less than when we were dating. And it wasn't long before I got tired of always being the one to start the fire. Instead of constantly initiating, I got used to "taking care of business" myself— and it was fine. *That's what happens when you get married,* I told myself. I talked myself out of feeling discontented. Besides, it was just a rough patch.

A year later, we decided it was time to have a baby. I got pregnant on my first try that summer. Christopher seemed shocked, maybe even disappointed, that I had gotten pregnant so quickly.

"You know those tests aren't always accurate," he said when I handed him the pink stick with the two blue lines.

"They're plenty accurate," I replied. "This is the same kind they use at my doctor's office."

"Well, this is going to change everything," he said as he disappeared up the stairs.

No kidding, I thought.

I gave him a few minutes alone, and then went upstairs to find him.

"You okay?" I asked.

"Yeah. Oh yeah, of course," he said. I could tell he was reading the look of worry on my face. "I'm just, well, surprised. I thought it would take a few tries."

"It can. But it just didn't with us, I guess."

"Must mean it's meant to be, huh?" He reached out to hug me.

"I'd like to think so." He told me he loved me and admitted that he was scared. I told him I was scared, too. We agreed that we'd tackle it together. It was what we wanted. I knew it was what I wanted, and I had no reason to doubt him when he echoed my desire to start a family. I felt good. I felt ready. And, honestly, I felt happy.

i had a difficult pregnancy. I fluctuated
between hunger and nausea, without a break from either. Eating became my only pastime. That and watching bad daytime TV. Christopher and I had sex only once during my entire pregnancy. He finally admitted that it freaked him out to do it while I was pregnant.

"It's too weird," he said.

"You mean I'm too fat," I responded angrily. At that point, it didn't matter what the reason was, really. I was pissed, and our sexualities seemed more incompatible than ever. I felt hurt and confused. I was doing this wonderful thing that we both wanted so much, and yet it made me unattractive to him. It was hard for me to articulate my feelings, though, because my moods were so dramatic and changing constantly. On good days, I accepted that Christopher just felt weird about it. It felt weird to me, too; It was hard to feel sexy when I was feeling so awkward. On bad days, I wondered what I was thinking by having a baby with someone whom I felt completely sexually incompatible with.

After our daughter was born, I was uncomfortably heavy, weighing more than I ever had in my life. I couldn't fit into anything, and often wore the scrubs Christopher had been given at the hospital when I had my emergency C-section.

I struggled with my weight for the next year, and Christopher and I never had sex. I didn't feel the least bit desirable, and without my prodding him, what little interest Christopher did have in sex disappeared completely.

I finally joined Weight Watchers to get back on track, but even after I lost weight, Christopher continued to struggle with the idea of our having sex. It was as if he simply couldn't look at me the way he had before I had the baby, and he seemed to have no libido at all.

"You just . . . you still look pregnant to me," he said one night. His comment sent me into a tailspin. I was angry at him, angry at myself. I was incredibly unhappy with the way I looked, too, and I felt awful, as if I were dragging my body along with me wherever I went. I kept hoping it would just pop back into shape, or that I would simply wake up one day and feel perfectly fine with the sagging belly and weighty thighs that no amount of diet and exercise seemed to be able to reduce. But nothing changed.

Christopher's comment was horrible and hurtful, but it was also true. Should he have wanted me anyway? Maybe. But he didn't. And I had trouble blaming him entirely, because my attitude certainly wasn't helping the matter. Maybe if I had felt and acted desirable, I would have been attractive to him regardless. Through it all, I felt silly and upset with myself. What difference did it make what my body looked like? I was conscious enough of media messaging to know that social expectations were also partly at fault, that I was being blasted by images that made me want to look thin and stay young and unmarred by pregnancy. I had a healthy baby girl and a loving husband. What I needed, I decided, was to get over myself.

But knowing the source of my vanity didn't make my desire to look better any less powerful. It's a crummy paradox: We're not supposed to care about appearance, but we live in a world that values the way a person looks over nearly everything else. In her book *Full Frontal Feminism,* Jessica Valenti explains, "We're expected to be hot—but if we are, we're vain and stupid. And if we're not hot, we're useless. Kind of hard to get around."[2] So true, and I wasn't having any luck avoiding this dilemma. So I decided to accept the paradox for what it was, despite its unfortunate source, and do what felt right for me.

The very next day after Christopher told me I still looked pregnant to him, I called the amazing plastic surgeon who had worked on my nose when I was in college. I had been unhappy with the large, crooked version my family's genes had provided me with, and was thrilled with the one that Dr. Williams put in its place. So, when I decided to have liposuction and a tummy tuck, I dialed his number without hesitation. Vanity had taken over, but I was unhappy with my body not looking and feeling the way I was used to it looking and feeling. And the surgery had the desired results. I felt normal again. Our sex life improved, but only because I was feeling good enough to be the one to initiate sex again. We went right back to the vanilla sex that we had had before we got married, but with less frequency. I thought I could deal with it. I rationalized that sex wasn't that big a part of marriage.

Ultimately, though, it was big to me. I missed it, and not having it made me sad. I was also angry—at Christopher for not craving me sexually, and at myself for not being attractive enough to inspire such craving. And since I was now feeling good about my body again, I found myself blaming him more readily and less compelled to blame myself. I even thought about leaving. But everything else was fine. He was lovely to me and wonderful with the baby. Sex was really the only issue we were on opposing planets about, barring all the usual stuff couples and parents argue about, like whose turn it is to do the dishes, change the baby, walk the dog, or figure out what's for dinner. It was impossible for me to fathom that a marriage could end over sex.

As I began to examine the history of our sex life, I thought about what I had given up to be with Christopher. Getting engaged to him meant that my lifestyle of safe but relatively casual, open sexuality had come to an abrupt halt. And that way of life hadn't just been handed to me—I'd had to work at it. I'd made a conscious decision that that was the way I wanted to express my sexuality, and my experiences had validated me. But when he proposed and I said yes, I was buying into the idea of monogamy. In my marriage, I was making a pact with my husband, and with society, that he would be the only man—rather, the only person—I would ever sleep with again. And I went along with it, just like everyone does. I'd hung in for three years by that point. The early stages of love will do that for you.

And now we'd conceived a baby, and I was a new mother. I'd heard that new mothers often don't want to have sex, but I can't say that I had heard the same thing said about dads. Still, we were both overworked and sleep deprived, and so I continued to assess and reassess my needs, reminding myself all the while, *This happens to everyone; this is normal; this too will pass.* I could hear all of the conventional wisdom echoing in my ears. I convinced myself that everything I had learned about sex and about myself applied only to my single self, and that my married self was someone entirely different—and that this was right.

But I was dissatisfied, and I began to accept that I had been for quite some time. I was hungry not just for more in terms of the *amount* of sex I was having, but also for more in terms of the *kind* of sex I was having. I missed sex with women, rough sex, and role playing—all of the things that I simply was not going to get via sex with Christopher. I didn't feel like a married version of myself. I felt like someone else entirely, a person who was supposed to be molded by a marriage and by social expectations that didn't suit her at all.

and then I met Grace. And, like a flood

I couldn't control, the real me came rushing back. It happened one weekend when I was away at an artists' retreat. It was the winter after my daughter turned two. I was profoundly aware of and amazed by the conflict I was living with. I was happily married, other than the fact that I was not okay with our sex life. Being a wife and a mom made that point even harder to reconcile, because I felt like I wasn't supposed to want or be focused on sex anymore. I had had my slutty years, and now I was supposed to be over them.

The irony of the fact that we're not supposed to have sex until we get married, and that once we get married we're not supposed to be sexual, was eating away at me. And the fact that this is a well-recognized social phenomenon didn't make me feel any better. In her book *The Meaning of Wife,* Anne

Kingston explains, "But here is the catch-22: While marriage sanctioned female sexuality, women were seen to undergo a sexual muting when they became wives."[3] And there you have it—the ugly and impossible contradictions, which we are taught as girls, that follow us through life. But despite the societal "normalcy" of what I was experiencing, there was no question that that "something missing" was starting to feel like an overwhelming need I simply had to fill. After all, with my sexuality being as important as it was to my self-definition, I felt like I was beginning to shrivel without it.

The weekend I met Grace was during a time when I was already having crazy fantasies that I'd miraculously meet some beautiful woman with whom I could have a marvelous affair. Someone who craved me.

And, go figure, I found exactly what I was looking for. Grace had never been with a woman before. She was caught in a sexless and loveless marriage that was destroying her. Her story was so pitiful, it almost made me grateful for the kind of difficulty I was experiencing. No sex is one thing; no love or support is quite another.

She arrived late, bustling into dinner with apologies and explanations. "How many times have I been here?" she said to everyone and no one in particular. "And still, I get lost every time." She charmed me immediately. She was a deeply intelligent but incredibly scattered woman with fair, freckled skin and long, curly hair that refused to cooperate with the clip she tried to hold it back in.

That night, Grace and I found ourselves alone on the porch after the group of women we'd been talking to had retired to bed. We sat in wooden rockers, looking up at the winter sky, and talked about everything and nothing. We were only four hours from home, but I felt like I was a million miles away from my life. The retreat was at a historic home that had been turned into a bed-and-breakfast, and the whole experience reminded me of a kind of commune, which I sometimes fantasized about living on—full of artistic, thinking women, all working together and supporting one another.

Grace and I started talking about love and sex and relationships and marriages.

"My husband has never made me come," she told me that night. It felt clear from that moment forward that we were going to end up sleeping together. How could that be? I wonder now. How could I have felt so ready for and open to cheating? And though what I did was nothing short of cheating, I somehow felt that Christopher wouldn't take it as badly—if he were to find out—because she was a woman, not a man. It's funny where our minds go when we're determined to rationalize something we desperately want to do but know we shouldn't.

As soon as Grace and I kissed, I actually felt relieved because my anxious urge had been quelled. Yet I also felt guilty for betraying my husband, and terrified that he would find out. Simultaneously, I thought that being with Grace would make me able to love Christopher better. It might sound as if I was making excuses for my behavior again, but I really wasn't. And I continue to stand by my reasoning. It turned out I was more fulfilled with Christopher when I was with Grace, because I no longer wanted something from him that he simply couldn't give me.

One of my interview subjects, a forty-year-old woman named Ella, said this about her open relationship: "We both know we can't be everything to each other, and we'd rather not be." Many people who are in open relationships come to this conclusion. But Ella's primary partner knows about her outside relationship, and at that point, mine did not.

I imagined my affair with Grace as a roadside stop, the kind you make to refuel and regenerate. I felt so good when I was with her. She loved my body. She loved making me feel good. And she loved that I could and wanted to do the same for her. I envisioned getting my strength back through my relationship with Grace, and then returning to my marriage, committed to working harder to be "happy" within socially prescribed confines. At the time, I had no idea what a contradiction that sentiment really was.

In *Against Love,* Laura Kipnis explains, "When it comes to love, trying is always too hard."[4] But at the time, it was that self-delusion that kept me going. After all, I was better at being with Christopher while I was with Grace. My resentment and anger about his ignoring my sexuality disappeared, and I enjoyed being with him, taking care of our daughter together, and being all the other parts of me that I am, too. But I was still struggling with how to have both things—how to maintain an outside relationship and be happy at home. I never imagined that doing so could actually translate into a lifestyle that would work for Christopher and me. Loving more was helping me to love more, not less, yet it still seemed impossible to merge my two lives, and the idea of being in an open marriage still hadn't crossed my mind. I had no idea what an open marriage was. All I knew was that I was having an affair, and that eventually either that or my marriage had to end.

Because Grace and I lived in the same city, we saw each other as often as we could. She was terrified that her husband would find out, and she'd convinced herself that he would because of me. I have no clue why, since she knew I had just as much to lose and no reason to reveal our relationship. She was freaked out that either I was going to tell her husband, or someone would see us or know about us and tell him.

In the end, she was the one who told him.

"I thought it would turn him on," she told me on the phone the next day. She was crying, and her voice was shaky. She sounded scared.

"And clearly, it didn't."

"No. He's furious . . . at you."

"At me?"

"He's convinced that you were the one who put me up to this, that I would have never done something like this without being pushed. He wants to talk to you."

"No," I said emphatically. "Absolutely not."

"You have to, or else he's going to tell Christopher."

"Shit," I said, feeling the weight of what I'd been avoiding. I think I truly believed that I could simply be with Grace for a while, until some natural fizzling-out point, much like the experience I had had with Sophie Anne. The last thing I wanted was to hurt Christopher. While Grace was talking, I realized what I had risked. *Christopher might leave me,* I thought. But in that same instant, I knew I didn't believe he really would. He would be sad about the choice I had made, but I also felt sure that we could survive.

I felt confident about this outcome in part because things were so good—better than they had been. I was happy and relaxed. And I felt certain that Grace and I could continue our relationship without having to end our marriages. Why couldn't we? Our routine was so easy to maintain because of our circumstances: Because Grace had a child, our kids could play together while we spent time talking. We were never intimate when the kids were around. We would just talk and watch them play. We planned our alone time together for certain evenings, when her husband was out or mine opted for an early night at home with our daughter. It was surprisingly easy to balance it all. In a lot of ways, my relationship with Grace felt more like an intimate friendship than anything else. I spent as much time with her as I did with any best friend I'd ever had. I loved Grace and I loved my husband, and it worked. The problem was that I was keeping it a secret, and that didn't work. I hated lying, and when I was confronted with telling the truth, I was terrified of how Christopher would feel about me.

After Grace told me her husband was demanding to talk to me, there was a painful silence as she waited for me to answer. But I didn't feel as if I had much choice in the matter, so I agreed. I agreed to talk to her husband, even though all I really wanted was for the whole situation to just disappear. That night, Grace's husband called me at home. I was as ready for him as I could be.

"I have things I'd like to say to you in person," he told me. I suggested we meet at his house the next day. When I arrived the next morning, Grace was there, cowering in the background, skittering in and out of the room, getting ready for work while her husband and I sat knee to knee in their living room. The conversation didn't go well. He started it by calling me a slut, and things went downhill from there.

When you decide to cheat, you choose to accept the consequences of being found out—and they are not likely to be positive. People who are being cheated on are generally not happy, although on certain occasions, the partner who's being cheated on is relieved, or, at the very least, not surprised. A Salon.com article by Carol Lloyd describes just such a situation. Lloyd writes, "The first time my husband confessed to cheating on me, I began giggling like an idiot. 'My God!' I cried. 'You promise?' I was giddy with relief to find we both had dipped into the same shallow philandering waters: making out with ex-lovers while out of town. We lay in bed and gently tormented one another . . . finally tiptoeing into a new understanding."[5]

Lloyd's experience is unusual only in that she and her spouse were able to share and discuss the fact that they were cheating on each other. But it's more likely that you will end up with a very unhappy, and perhaps very angry, person on your hands when you confess to an indiscretion. Cheating by its very nature is about deceit, and no one likes to be deceived. And being the deceiver comes with its own host of issues—namely guilt.

Delia, a twenty-year-old woman in an open civil union in New Zealand, describes her experiences with cheating: "Prior to becoming polyamorous, I was in three long-term monogamous relationships. I cheated on both the first and second, and was cheated on by the third. I felt immense guilt over the first ones." Via email, Delia told me that she felt guilty "mostly for feeling bad about not feeling bad!"

Liza, another interview subject, also talked about the effect that cheating has had on her life. Even though she has never cheated, both of her parents did. "I saw how incredibly destructive it can be, and how devastating it is on the other partner," she told me.

Aside from the fact that I wasn't considering an open relationship at that point, Grace's husband was an extremely jealous man who did not like the idea of sharing his wife with me. He was also controlling and selfish. He needed to own Grace. Her primary complaint about him was that she felt like his property, and not particularly highly valued property at that. But he didn't see that. He believed his obsession with possessing her was a sign of his love for her. Many people make that mistake, and it's always the person being possessed who suffers the most.

As angry as Grace's husband was—and he was *angry*—I know things would have been far worse if I had been a man. It's ridiculous, but it's fitting in a culture that still values men over women, and in which lesbian sex isn't seen as "real" sex. I was an annoyance to him, but not a threat. It seemed to me that he should have been far *more* threatened that I was a woman, simply by virtue of the fact that I was able to give Grace everything that was missing from their relationship. Perhaps, if he'd been a different person, he could have grasped how my being in Grace's life might have helped their marriage. But, of course, that wasn't how he saw things.

Our six-month affair ended in disaster. For Grace it challenged too much, involved too many risks, and introduced too many questions, but for me our relationship was an opening, an awakening. I'd been ignoring what I wanted and needed. In my marriage, I'd simply accepted things as they were, without regard for how I was feeling. Herein lies the rub: If, out of the blue, you have an experience that not only wakes you up, but also reminds you of what you used to enjoy, it's tricky to go back to sleep. This type of encounter can challenge all those beliefs you have come to accept as normal. It upsets the life you were living, because it opens a door that can't be shut easily. And it forces you to rely on yourself and ask yourself what your truth is. When your experiences counter your beliefs but also feel so right, you can get yourself into a very confusing place, one that takes some working through to figure out how to handle it.

And that's where I found myself. My affair with Grace started me thinking about the nature of sexuality, and questioning the institution of marriage altogether. It wasn't that I hadn't thought about it before. I've always been a big reader of everything from feminist manifestos to literary erotica. I take *Cosmo* quizzes and read *The Hite Report*. I've read Anaïs Nin and Camille Paglia. But I'd never let myself seriously consider the ramifications of my sexuality on the life I was living. It was like this ever-looming disconnect. But rather than living my truth, I'd just allowed myself to believe that I was a freak for the sexual feelings I had, and for liking sex without necessarily connecting it with love. Rather than accepting that my tendencies might be incompatible with traditional married life, I mistakenly believed that I was strong enough to overcome them, or at least live with ignoring them. But I couldn't.

Being with Grace reminded me of how much I liked sex, desired women, and was attracted to men other than my husband. It was as simple as that: She had forced me out of my comatose state. I was no longer going through my daily life with my body in motion and my mind on pause, because, if I was honest with myself, I cared about honoring my sexuality. Before that, I'd been wrestling with the idea that my desires were not being met, but that it was my fault: I was too fat; I was a mom and thus no longer sexy; my husband had fallen out of love with me. But none of those excuses held up: I lost the weight; I felt sexy; Christopher made it clear again and again that he loved me for me. Really, the issue was much bigger, and it had to be addressed head on if I was ever going to feel happy in my marriage. There was just no way around it.

i was shaking when I got home from

Grace's house that day. I was sad and angry and I had no idea what was going to happen, but I knew I had to tell Christopher about the affair.

"But why?" he said when I told him. "Why?"

"You don't want me. I thought you'd be happy," I said. But that was putting the blame on him, which, as easy as it would have been, was not what I wanted to do. I changed the conversation's course almost instantly. "I'm not happy," I confessed. My morning with Grace's husband had left me mad and resentful and scared, but I needed to be honest, too. I wanted to beg Christopher's forgiveness, but I also wanted to scream at him, *This is your fault, you asshole! Why don't you want to have sex with me anymore?* But it wasn't just about that: I also wanted to be with other people. I wanted different experiences, different relationships, different kinds of sex.

"I don't know how you can say that, Jenny. I do love you."

"I know you love me, but do you want me?"

"Of course I want you." He put his hand on my thigh, and I brushed it away.

"It sure doesn't feel like it."

We continued to talk well into the night. We talked about whether this meant we would leave each other, but neither of us wanted that. He wanted things to be the same and I wanted things to be different, but we still wanted to be with each other.

"We have to do better than this," I told him. "This isn't working. I'm happy with nearly every other aspect of our marriage, but I'm miserable about our sex life."

He apologized and promised it would be better, that he would be more attentive. I've heard this time and time again from women, but, sadly, it's often too late by the time a couple gets to this point in their marriage. I was willing to give it a shot, but my eyes had been opened, my awakening had been abrupt, and I liked what I saw on the other side. I wanted those possibilities. And yet I struggled because I wasn't ready to leave Christopher, either.

I had told him before we got engaged that I had been with women before. I had a feeling he might propose, and I wanted him to know everything about me. He seemed pretty blasé about it at the time. "But once we decide it's just you and me, then it's just you and me," he said. It wasn't a question. "Of course," I replied, and at the time I meant it wholeheartedly. But I still cheated on him, because I felt desperate. I just wanted to stop the flood of feelings I had, feelings of being sexless, like "Mommy" was all I was now. I don't know that I felt this at the time, but in retrospect, my infidelity may have put my marriage into a state of sink or swim. Something had to give, and cheating was potentially going to save us. It was a sort of last resort, a means to an end. I understand, of course, that that didn't, and still doesn't, make it right.

There we were, this clichéd couple with a baby and a house and a life. And here I was, coming out of a relationship that had stirred me, made me feel alive in a way I hadn't in such a long time. Despite feeling scared and stressed out all the time about being found out, I also couldn't help but think about how Grace made me feel. Why was I having such intense feelings for her? Should I have been having those feelings for someone else when I was married? Was it possible that I didn't want my marriage to end, even though I wanted—needed—to be with other people?

I longed to be normal, to be content like the women I saw around me. I wanted a household that looked like my vision of everyone else's, with their happy, healthy, successful marriages. But then I realized that lots of people *look* like that from the outside. Hell, we did. And yet I knew that affairs were on the rise, especially among women.

Locating hard statistics on affairs in the United States is difficult at best. Studies don't often elicit honest answers and are often found flawed and biased in both design and execution. I found statistics stating that anywhere from 12 percent to nearly 70 percent of women cheat. Anecdotally, there's evidence of these higher numbers in a bevy of successful websites that facilitate cheating, and magazine headlines about women who stray. Some websites and books are devoted to helping people find out if their spouses are cheating, and other resources discuss how to cheat and how to recover from infidelity.

As I mulled all of this over, I kept coming back to the question of monogamy. *Are there really any happy, successful marriages?* I asked myself. I started to wonder how many of the people I passed on the street every day were cheating on their partners. I started wondering if I could stay married to Christopher and still see other people. What would that really look like? At first, I just thought there was no way. I'd be too jealous. Christopher would be too jealous. It would be too complicated. Where would we meet people? How would we know they were safe? Would they only be people from out of town? What if we met someone in town? Would we have threesomes? Foursomes? Would we go to "parties"? Would I sleep just with other women, or men, too? Would it just be sex, or would I fall in love? The more I thought about it, the more confused I became, and not just because of the ins and outs of how something like this might or might not work out. There was also the question of whether any of it even made sense. I vacillated between three ways of thinking about my marriage: 1) This was "just the way it was," and I should deal with it; 2) I had married the wrong person; and 3) I had married the right person, but I could stay with him only if I could also have the freedom to be with other people.

as I often do when I find myself in a philosophical quandary of sorts, I finally decided to talk to my dad about my conflict. Although having a rabbi as a father can be tough at times, it can also be wonderfully convenient. I can and do talk to him about my life and the world at large. That is no less true when it comes to issues of love, sex, and relationships. Over the years, my dad has made it clear that he finds marriage, as well as a number of other societal conventions, deeply flawed at best. So, even though it made me a little uneasy to confide in my own father about this particular issue, I decided I needed his input. And I told him everything.

He took it all in, and then he likened what was going on with me to Christmas, believe it or not. "People imagine marriage is just like Christmas," he explained. "They have this image of what it *should* be, and yet that was never the reality and can't be the reality. Yes, some people have lovely Christmases, complete with carols and relatives. But even those family gatherings aren't the perfect, Rockwellesque events that people long for. They drag their kids to the mall to sit on a fat, old stranger's lap so they can tell him their wishes. Christmas is built around fantasy. It doesn't matter that the kids are miserable, or that the mom is exhausted, or that the father would rather watch the game than eat the meal his wife slaved over all day. But you're not allowed to say that. You have to play along, or else you ruin it for everyone else."

We continued to discuss human nature and how we behave when we're attempting to be part of a cohesive society. My dad entered rabbi mode, as he often does during such conversations: no judgments, just thinking. I commented on the paradox that exists when we try to live in a way that strikes me as antithetical to human nature—that is, how popular monogamous marriage is, despite the fact that our biology does not necessarily seem compatible with that way of life. The question is, why would we prolong our silence and discomfort about something so important that affects so many people?

"For a couple of reasons," my father told me. "Misery loves company. You can't go off and do your own thing and be happy. You had better feel guilty, and you had better be prepared to be labeled as the weirdo that you are. Everyone loves Christmas, and that's an order. It's the same way with marriage. This is how it's done, and it doesn't matter that not many people are happy, or that the human body and mind aren't suited to monogamous marriage. That's the way it is, and that's the way it shall be. And anyone who dares to go off and do their own thing will be shot. Better right than happy."

"Do you really believe that? Really?"

"I do."

I wasn't surprised. Over the previous ten years, my father had begun to combine his education in the Jewish tradition with Buddhist teachings. He now believes in living life awake, not living it for others.

"So, you don't believe in monogamous marriage?" I asked.

"People aren't built for it, and we never lived that way until very recent history. People love to pound the Bible when they want to defend their righteous ways, but they should have another look at it. People have long lived in communities and groups. Men had lovers or concubines or multiple wives. Kings and queens kept their own apartments. Women of status had lovers, and sometimes even servants, to service them. What do you imagine that was about? Marriage was about money and property, and not about love." He went on to explain that he believed we act outwardly like we cleave to the current model because it's what's been done for as long as people can remember. However, we don't actually live that way, obviously. People have mistresses and lovers and simply choose to lie about their behavior, rather than face their own hypocrisy.

"And to change it all?" I asked.

"It'll take a revolution," my father said, "because change doesn't come easy, and people don't like it."

So, despite the misery in many marriages, the fact that the marriage exists (and will, theoretically, continue to exist—even if only in all its miserable glory) can apparently be comforting. And even people in the most stifling and static marriages often convince themselves that the relationship is working, and that they have no good reason to rock the boat. Iris Krasnow, in her horrifyingly antifeminist book *Surrendering to Marriage,* actually suggests that women keep paddling away because "perhaps being happy in marriage is not what we should be seeking after all."[6] What should we expect instead? According to Krasnow, marriage requires women to surrender themselves to their husbands, and to "tortuous work and predictable routine."[7] And yet women are expected to accept this setup—not because it's logical, but instead because it's prevalent. Krasnow's argument may be insane, but her viewpoint on marriage is not uncommon. Women want to feel validated in their unhappiness so they can ignore their own circumstances and go along with the status quo. And Krasnow gives them just that incentive.

I've thought many times since that day about what my father and I talked about. That conversation was what helped me—though it took some time—to finally feel confident that I was neither crazy nor an anomaly. I was terribly and unsurprisingly normal. But I still decided to give my marriage the old college try. Even with the support and guidance of someone like my father, I am still a product of the society I was born into, whether I like it or not. And I did know people who were happily married, or so both partners claimed. Surely it was possible. Why else would so many people keep attempting such relationships? And what about all of the romantic books and movies out there? There had to be some truth to them, right?

From cradle to grave, we are conditioned to believe that marriage is the be-all and end-all of this thing called life—that it is a sign of our success or failure. And so, when you're in a functioning marriage, it's pretty tough to explain to people that somehow, it's not "working" for you. But there I was, thinking that maybe I wanted to stay in my marriage *and* see other people.

I decided that I did believe in love, and in the union Christopher and I had formed. And, quite honestly, I was feeling too overwhelmed by the social messages I had received to do anything other than hunker down and figure out if we could make our situation work. I had no model for the type of arrangement I was just beginning to piece together in my head, so I chose to shelve it and focus on giving my marriage another go. We had committed to this. We had a kid. What else was there to do?

Chapter 4
everyone else manages to do it, why can't i?

She made a pact with herself to try to be what was expected of her. They moved to a planned community, and she baked brownies and volunteered at her daughter's school. She hosted happy hours and wore sundresses. But she couldn't keep it up. Her marriage couldn't last the way it was. She thought maybe she had married the wrong guy, or that maybe she was a lesbian. She thought perhaps she just needed to have lovers outside of her marriage. Talking to her husband about what she needed was the only way to figure it out. It was the hardest thing she'd ever have to do, but she had to try.

after I had decided to recommit to my marriage, Christopher and I moved to a planned community called The Estates. We built our dream house, handpicking

the paint, the doorknobs, and every possible household fix-
ture and appliance. We carefully planned where the electrical
outlets and towel bars would go. I threw myself into that
house and the move with a passion unlike anything I'd ever
experienced for something so wholly material. Not until later
did I realize how much that energy was about my commitment to turning myself into a "good wife." I was sure that I
was the problem, after all. I had only myself to blame. I had
been lazy. I hadn't fully invested myself in my husband and
my family. I could do a better job—all I had to do was work
harder, and building the perfect house in the perfect neighborhood seemed like a great place to start.

I was quite happy for a while when we first moved to
The Estates. The house was indeed everything I had always
wanted, the neighborhood was beautiful, and everything
was within arm's reach. The built-in community seemed to
provide a solution for what I was lacking. I had a toddler at
home and only a few friends left from my graduate school
days. I wanted married friends with children, friends whose
lives paralleled—or at least seemed to parallel—my own.
These women, my new neighbors, all seemed to be doing
the wife thing so well. I figured if I could just blend in and
be like them, all my problems would be solved.

I went to all of the playgroups, moms'-nights-out
events, neighborhood happy hours, gourmet club dinners,
and candle parties. I took up scrapbooking. And I enjoyed
myself. It felt like summer camp, which, barring that

summer when Brian had stomped on my heart, I'd always loved. I made a handful of close friends and lots more acquaintances. It actually seemed as if I had found my place. But, as generally happens when you're trying hard to be the person you're not, the whole façade started to unravel little by little. I was pretending to be happy, and no amount of willing myself to be different was going to change the fact that I wasn't.

Inevitably, the novelty wore off. Too many of the women talked about nothing other than their window treatments and their children when they weren't complaining about their lives and their husbands. A number of these women had had high-powered jobs before they'd had children and moved to The Estates. Now they were nursemaids and ladies who lunched.

I was basically a stay-at-home mom myself. Although I was teaching full-time at night, I was mommying all day long. Many of the women in The Estates had given up nearly everything that had previously defined them—their jobs, their non-mommy friends, their hobbies—in exchange for a big house in the burbs and annual trips to Tahiti. But all the status in the world couldn't hide the fact that these women were prisoners in their own lives: Some even had to ask permission to go out at night, and when their husbands were with the kids, both spouses referred to it as "baby-sitting."

Some of the husbands traveled more than half the year, and when they were home, they were often mowing the lawn or golfing. Meanwhile, their wives dutifully kept the home fires burning. Many of my new friends were lonely and sad, and others had that sleepwalking thing going on, smiles plastered in place. Wasn't this the life they'd fought so hard for? Yet they had to smile to hold it all together—and some of us had to wonder how we'd ended up here.

"The housewife is more an invention of privileged people in ranked societies than a natural role of human animal," writes Helen Fisher in *Anatomy of Love*.[1] It certainly felt like an undesirable, false role to me at the time. And while I'd like to believe that the modern-day housewife role is somehow based on good intentions, it's just not working out for most women. *Now what?* they too often wonder. Nothing staves off reality like a damn good brownie.

What about me? was the question I was asking myself. The trade-off was supposed to be some divine sense of fulfillment that only wifedom and motherhood could bring me, but, despite my high hopes, I was coming up short.

I know some women can manage this lifestyle, and I understand that some parts of it can be very rewarding. But at what cost? Certainly, it varies from woman to woman, and for some, it's not even a question. But, looking at the preponderance of women in my new community, I couldn't help but wonder how I'd ended up in Stepford, surrounded by so many unhappy women who shopped and gossiped to fill their tiresome days. From my vantage point, there seemed to be two types of women in The Estates: those who had forgotten who they were and what they wanted, and were resigned to that fact (even content about it), and those who were unhappy but saw no alternative. When they complained about their situations, they often followed by saying, "But it is what it is."

"I signed up for this, I guess," they'd tell me. They'd lament the fact that their husbands didn't want to have sex with them anymore, or that their husbands wanted to have sex too often. Some talked about their spouses' wanting to do "weird" stuff. When I listened to what some of those requests were—things like spanking—I actually found them fairly benign. One woman confessed that she was mortified that her husband had asked her to try some new positions.

"Why don't you want to try it?" I asked.

"What do you mean, 'why?'"

"I mean, how do you know you won't like it?"

"It's what sluts do," she pronounced solemnly.

"Really?" I replied. I must have sounded a bit too incredulous, because she raised her eyebrows and gave me an expectant look.

"I like to have sweet, romantic sex, too," I told her, "but I also like to talk dirty and play rough sometimes." I wasn't totally alone among my new friends, I soon found out, as sex turned out to be one of our most frequent topics of conversation once we opened that door.

i did become very close with three or

four women in the neighborhood, particularly with one named Samantha. She had a great sex life with her husband, Clayton. She talked about the wild places they'd done it, and how they took vacations just to have sex without fear of being interrupted by one of their three kids. She would become one of the few friends with whom I felt connected enough to discuss my ideas about open marriage. She admitted she was attracted to other people, and her husband had told her on more than one occasion that he'd love to have a threesome.

"I'd be too jealous if I saw him with another woman, though," she told me. "I'm not into women. I've thought about it, but I just don't think I could go through with it." She knew I'd been with women, and I'd even suggested flirtatiously a few times, just to test the waters, that we get together. She always laughed off my advances; she was never uncomfortable, but never interested, either. It was a relief to have a friend whom I could be completely honest with, and who didn't think I was a freak. Nothing I could tell her would bother her, because Samantha and Clayton had an interesting sex life of their own, which they worked constantly to keep new and exciting. They bought a massage table for their bedroom, had a chest full of sex toys, and had sex with a frequency I envied.

Despite all of that—a seemingly ideal scenario that I wished Christopher and I could have—Clayton struck me as someone who might still be interested in having other partners. He loved and was satisfied with Samantha, and I cannot imagine he ever would have cheated on her. But I couldn't help but wonder if he might be open to experimenting with other people if Samantha herself were open to it. They certainly didn't hide the fact that they found other people attractive. His desire didn't seem to bother her. She found it quite natural, and would often say that as long as he didn't act on it, it didn't present a problem in their relationship.

I have admired Samantha and Clayton's partnership since we first met. They are the reason why I continue to believe that monogamy, although I see it as a choice, can work for the right couple.

That's not to say that the idea of "venturing out" hasn't crossed either of their minds at one point or another. One night, a group of couples from our neighborhood were out to dinner. We had to wait for our table, so we all settled in at the bar—women at one end, men at the other. My husband, usually in an effort to combat his shyness, has a tendency to pose clever questions in group settings. "If you could have any superpower," he asked the men, "what would it be?" Not surprisingly, most of the guys wanted to be able to read people's minds or see into the future. But not Clayton. Laughing drunkenly, he actually told the three other men standing there that he wished for the ability to sleep with other women without his wife finding out.

When Christopher told me about Clayton's remark that night, I wasn't shocked. I was kind of surprised that he had said it out loud, in front of his wife's friends' husbands, but I was also glad about that, because it implied that he wouldn't care if Samantha knew. It made me think that he would've made the same comment in front of Samantha, and that felt like awfully good couple honesty to me. More than anything, though, I was relieved that I wasn't alone. It was too easy to think I wanted something more just because I was dissatisfied, or just because I wanted more, period. I felt an unspoken camaraderie with Clayton, but I never let either him or Samantha know that Christopher had shared Clayton's superpower wish with me.

Six months went by, and Samantha and I began spending more time together. One day, she was dropping me off at my house after one of our bimonthly girls' nights out at the local bar. As I said goodbye, just as I was pushing the car door open, she turned to me and said, "Clayton wants you for his birthday." She was a little drunk. I could tell she was teasing, but I knew there was an element of truth there, and that she was curious about how I would respond.

"Excuse me?" I said, letting the door close again and settling back into my seat.

"He's turning forty next month, you know? And when I asked him what he wanted for his birthday, he said he wanted another woman to join us in bed, and that he'd like that other woman to be you."

"Wow," I said. That was all I had. We sat in silence. It wasn't awkward, exactly, but I think I was as interested to hear her reaction as she was to hear mine. "So . . . " I prompted, after I couldn't take the silence any longer.

"So, I don't know," she said. "Would you?"

"You know I've wanted to sleep with you since the minute I met you," I said. She'd heard it a million times by that point, and she still wasn't interested. I had noticed that sometimes, after she'd had a drink or two, she'd start to get flirty, but I still didn't think sealing the deal was part of her plan.

"Shut up," she said lightheartedly. "I know. But what about Clayton?"

"I'd be willing to take my medicine to get my sugar." This came out before I even knew what I'd said. I was flirting with her because I wanted to see where it would go, but I wasn't sure that I would have gone through with it, either. It was too close to home. I wasn't interested in Clayton, and I wouldn't have wanted to risk a friendship that continues, even today, to be a huge part of my life.

"Well, you never know," she said, which is what she always said when I'd feigned a proposition. I got out of the car and made my way up to my front door. When I turned around, she was still sitting there, and we waved goodbye again. I felt conflicted, not because I believed anything would ever happen between Samantha and me, or Samantha and Clayton and me, but because she was opening a window on an option I felt like I wanted to have with Christopher. Here was this sexually satisfied couple who entertained the thought of opening their relationship, even if only for a one-time thing. Amid all of these other couples who seemed so out of step with each other, Samantha and Clayton were completely attuned, and yet no amount of sexual satisfaction seemed to cancel out their natural desire for other partners.

Their marriage was a revelation to me. Most people do want something new and different, but the question is whether they can be honest about it, instead of repressing their urges or cheating. When I thought about Clayton and Samantha's relationship, it hit me all over again: It's not about sex; it's about honesty. And what could be healthier than that? They were living proof that even the happiest and most sexually satisfied couples aren't immune to outside desires.

These ideas were stirring in my head, but I still wasn't prepared to suggest anything to Christopher just yet. After all, talking about those impulses and acting on them were two very different things. My desire existed—that was clear. The honesty part seemed like a great idea, and I was all for it. But could we really sleep with other people and still be okay?

Samantha and Clayton were certainly more the exception than the rule, after all, and not just in my neighborhood, but also in my experience at large. A couple that better exemplified the kind of relationships I tended to encounter was Elizabeth and her husband, Brian. Their marriage was problematic on many different levels, entrenched as it had been, for as long as I'd known them, in a modern tragedy of the virgin/whore variety. That dichotomy, in which the male half of a partnership wants a kitten in the kitchen and a tiger in the bedroom, is incredibly emotionally draining and confusing for women, whether they're married or not. It leaves them with the near-impossible task of negotiating the untenable space of being a good girl with a nasty streak, the kind of girl you can take home to Mama *and* who is sexual— but not too sexual. Too often, it happens that men find that nasty girl and then expect her to suppress her behavior a bit after she's married. And once kids are in the picture, she's gotta tone it *waaaay* down.

I think this is a predicament many couples struggle with—the question of how "slutty" a woman is "allowed" to be, and how much of a nasty girl a husband wants in his wife. Even simply laying out the idea exemplifies how much of a double standard it is to begin with. A man experiences no similar pressure. He can pretty much set the tone for the relationship, and even if his wife complains that he's sexually deviant—looking at porn, frequenting strip clubs, cheating—she's still the one who's trying to figure out how to satisfy him, how to make the marriage happy. For me, the sexual issues surrounding being someone's wife led me to consider the idea of open marriage, but for other couples, like Elizabeth and Brian, this sexual disconnect I've just described only continued to fester until it became a palpable problem that infested every other part of their lives.

One night early on in Christopher's and my friendship with Elizabeth and Brian, we were at a neighborhood dinner party. Some twenty other people were milling about, but only a half a dozen or so were within earshot. Brian approached me and, apropos of nothing, said, "You would never have been in Elizabeth's sorority."

"Why's that?" I asked.

"You would have been in the sorority of the girls guys slept with. Elizabeth was in the sorority of the girls guys married."

Brian's comment had no context; he wasn't even drunk. He had simply decided it would be okay, in that moment, to launch into a diatribe about his perception of my sexuality versus his wife's. And he didn't stop there. He went on to tell me how Elizabeth had been a virgin when they got married, and had purportedly lost all interest in sex not too far into their marriage. Surprise, surprise. Brian had a reputation for spewing distasteful comments about his wife. I remembered one occasion when he had told a group of neighbors, "I can't get my wife to fuck me, no matter what I buy her."

I always felt like asking him, "And what did you expect when you married her?" He wanted to marry a virgin, and he got one. And as far as she was concerned, she'd done the right thing: She'd followed the rules and gotten the guy, and then—partly because he wanted her to be someone else, and partly because he had always been someone other than who he professed to be—she couldn't stand him, and he couldn't stand her. She molded herself into the woman society said (and Brian agreed) she was supposed to be, only to get the backhanded message that her uptight ways were boring and priggish.

It was sad and painful to watch Elizabeth. She worked her tail off to run the perfect household. Her home was always spotless, her children always looked adorable, and I never saw her looking unkempt in the slightest. Eventually, she caved in to her husband's demands. She started wearing low-slung jeans and low-cut shirts, instead of the more conservative clothing she preferred. But their issues never really stemmed from something as simple as wardrobe disagreements—they were always about intent. Elizabeth's intent was to be the perfect wife and mother, as defined by Hallmark, Disney, and Lifetime Television. Brian's intent was to marry that girl and, I guess, hope that a martian invasion would occur and Pamela Anderson's body and attitude would replace Elizabeth's. It was an unfair setup from the start.

Brian had pursued other women from the very beginning, including me. He once pulled me onto his lap in the back seat of their minivan while she was driving and Christopher was in the front seat. I played it off at the time, in an effort to protect Elizabeth's feelings. But finally, when I couldn't take it anymore, I confronted her with the fact that her husband's passes at me were making me uncomfortable. Our discussion marked the beginning of the end of our friendship.

"It has nothing to do with you. It's him," she told me. "He does this wherever we go. I hate it. I'd leave him if it weren't for the kids." So she enabled him. And when our friendship took a quick nosedive after that conversation, I realized that cutting me out of the picture was the only way Elizabeth knew how to cope. I was crushed. She had been a good friend and a lovely person stuck in a rotten situation, and she and I both got the short end of the stick.

I imagine that part of what Elizabeth couldn't deal with was her realization—along with the confirmation that I knew it and saw it—that I exemplified what Brian wanted. For me, dealing with being that woman—the one men want—is no easy task. It stems from the fact that I'm open about my sexuality. It means that I've had to put up with being labeled a slut for being sexually sure of myself and refusing to apologize for having a healthy interest in sex. And I'm not talking about junior high and high school—I've been treated this way by my well-educated, cultured, well-traveled adult neighbors in an upscale neighborhood.

Christopher and I never played out the virgin/whore dichotomy, perhaps because I was happy to be both the virgin and the whore, just like I had been before our marriage. There's nothing wrong with being and wanting to be both, as long as that urge comes from an authentic place and is not forced on you. I'm happy baking cookies—sometimes.

And I'm happy being dominant in bed—sometimes. Dealing with the mixed messages and the shoulds and should-nots surrounding relationships and sex is not about whether any given thing is right or wrong. It's about whether it works for the couple. I'm not talking about things that are quantifiably deviant, like bestiality or pedophilia or anything nonconsensual; I'm talking about two adults conducting their marriage honestly, in ways that are appropriate for them. If Elizabeth wanted to be only the "virgin" (truly wanted it, that is, rather than feeling compelled because of societal pressures about being a "good girl"), then why should she have been judged and demeaned, especially by a husband who knew exactly what he was getting into?

When I was friends with Elizabeth and Brian, I was already very confused about where my own marriage was heading. Surrounded by so many couples who seemed static, if not miserable, I'd look at myself with Christopher and think, *Hey, we're doing okay.* He did plenty around the house. He cooked and was an equal parent to Emily. I still felt like the primary housekeeper and childcare provider, but I had comparatively little to complain about. Even so, I was feeling terribly alone and undersexed. I wanted him to want to cuddle with me and watch romantic comedies and chat and dissect a single conversation for hours, and I wanted him to ravish me. I wanted it all.

Around that time, my suspicions that perhaps I'd married the wrong man, which I'd started having after I broke up with

Grace, began to creep back into my consciousness. Maybe if I had found my Prince Charming, I wouldn't be having this problem. But the most outstanding issue that plagued me, day in and day out, was my growing conviction that something was wrong with me. Here I was, with this guy who had all these great qualities, so why the hell couldn't I just be happy? I had what lots of women could only dream of. I knew by then that there was no such thing as having it all, so why couldn't I just be satisfied with having an awful lot? Maybe I was just some sort of aberration, or was simply impossible to please. Could it be that nothing would ever be enough for me? Was dissatisfaction simply my natural state of being?

When I shared my woes with my friends, they offered all kinds of additional reasons: Maybe I shouldn't have gotten married in the first place. Maybe I just wasn't the monogamous type. Maybe I was a lesbian. But whenever I considered what leaving my husband would actually mean, what finding and marrying another man might be like, or how spending my life with a woman would feel, I became more conflicted and unhappy. It wasn't that I wanted someone instead of my husband; I wanted something in addition to what we had, something that Christopher couldn't offer me. I was craving sexual freedom, an outlet for my sensual needs. And it was increasingly apparent, especially since he and I had had some heart-to-hearts about what each of us wanted, that I craved more than what Christopher or any other *one* person could provide for me—I wanted variety.

I began to think it was unfair—ludicrous, really—to expect my husband to fulfill me on every level. Outside of the bedroom, I don't have those standards for him. We have different friends for different things. I have friends with whom I go to social events and bars. I have friends to whom I turn when things get rough, even if I haven't spoken to them in months. I have friends I exercise with. Friends I shop with. Friends with whom I trade off childcare responsibilities. It's not like elementary school. I don't have one best friend; I have many dear friends. I'm lucky and grateful for that. And I have found amazing happiness in knowing whom to lean on when, and not mistaking my favorite drinking buddy with my soul-baring confidant. But the rules are different in the bedroom. When your partner isn't enough, there's no socially acceptable solution. You're expected to just deal with it. You're not supposed to (read: allowed to) go out and find someone else to take care of the things that aren't available, or that are lacking, or that you're missing. Of course, people do—many people, in fact—but they do so secretly and guiltily.

I spent a lot of time trying to process why I felt the way I did. I didn't have a strained or problematic relationship with my father. I wasn't sexually abused. I didn't think I had a particularly addictive personality. The more I talked to people about my dilemma, the less secure I felt that lots of other people out there were just like me. It was just the opposite, in fact. Why was I different? Too many male genes and bad movies? Too much porn? Or what if I was perfectly normal, but part of a group of women (or *people,* for that matter) who were just too afraid to admit to who they were and what they wanted? I didn't get too far into this train of thought before I realized that this group I'd identified includes nearly everyone—everyone who has ever thought, *I love my partner. I love our relationship. And I want to sleep with other people.*

As my attitude about my sex life got increasingly worse, my dissatisfaction spilled over into the rest of my life and affected everything I did. At the time, though, I wasn't self-aware enough to realize the full extent of what was going on. It should have been obvious: If you're having trouble at work, your family's affected. If you're having trouble with your spouse, your work's impacted. If you're having trouble with your kids, your relationships with your spouse and your work suffer. Everything in life is connected, and sex is no small part of that equation. But for me, it was one part that I believed I did—and should—have complete control over.

Part of my difficulty was that all the things I was mulling over were based on my own experiences, and I didn't have many friends I could share my thoughts with. Sadly, I felt scared about discussing them with Christopher. I didn't want him to think I was nuts, and I didn't want to lose him, especially if what I was going through was just a matter of realigning my brain and getting with the program. But too much evidence was telling me that getting with the program wasn't what I needed. So I decided to pursue that evidence and do more fact gathering.

My quest started with books about relationships and marriage, sexuality and monogamy. People look at marriage as the "right" choice, or, alternately, as a moral or good choice, because it's assumed that human beings will be monogamous upon committing to this arrangement. Of course, more than ample proof exists that marriage doesn't do much to enforce monogamy. "There is no question about monogamy's being natural. It isn't," writes David P. Barash in his book *The Myth of Monogamy: Fidelity and Infidelity in Animals and People.*[2] Science tells us that monogamy is not part of our biological makeup, yet we pursue it vehemently, even as people everywhere fail miserably at it. So why the wide-sweeping assumption? The answer is the same as it is for so many of life's big questions: That's just the way it is. There's a reason why Bruce Hornsby has sold so many albums.

The reality is that we have it all wrong. According to Barash, "before the cultural homogenization that came with Western colonialism, more than three-quarters of all human societies were polygynous."[3] The social order is what dragged us into this mess. Science writer Ker Than notes, "Of the roughly 5,000 species of mammals, only 3 to 5 percent are known to form lifelong pair bonds. This select group includes beavers, otters, wolves, some bats and foxes, and a few hoofed animals."[4] And even those mammals in monogamous pairs tend to practice social, rather than sexual, monogamy, as do the known monogamous creatures in other species.

It's not just the hard sciences that steer us away from the idea that monogamy is central to our existence; social science indicates it as well. My conversation with my father that night had launched me into a further investigation of what I already both knew and suspected about the origins of marriage. And though what I discovered only further proved that knowledge and those suspicions, I was happy for the reminder of just how far from the truth our commonly held conceptions about marriage really are, as it bolstered the arguments that had been ruminating in my head: Marriage was strictly about money until the last one hundred years, when romantic love was introduced into the equation. For most of history, "marriage was an economic and political transaction,"[5] explains researcher, author, and professor Stephanie Coontz in her book *Marriage, a History.* It wasn't about love or sex or finding The One. It was about creating family alliances and building a labor force to run the farm. "Only in the seventeenth century did a series of political, economic, and cultural changes in Europe begin to erode the older functions of marriage, encouraging individuals to choose their mates on the basis of personal affection."[6] Sexually monogamous marriages are relatively new, historically speaking, and anthropologists regard why they ever stuck as *the* social standard as a mystery, despite our blind adherence to its dictates. So it's not surprising that we're failing at the rate we are.

In *Against Love,* Kipnis gives credit to our pre–romantic marriage ancestors: "At least they didn't devote themselves to trying to sustain a fleeting experience past its shelf life or transform it into the basis of a long-term relationship."[7] This idea resonated with me completely. The problem wasn't with me; it was with the institution. The one-size-fits-no-one concept of marriage comes not from some longstanding tradition, but instead from . . . literature. "A number of historians consider our version of romantic love a learned behavior that became fashionable only in the late eighteenth century, along with the new fashion of novel reading,"[8] writes Kipnis.

People are in love with love. Any number of Hollywood blockbusters or *New York Times* bestsellers prove that undeniably. But does the concept actually represent how people truly do experience love? Sure, plenty of us manage to fall in love. But just how sustainable is that fairytale high? Most of us can point to examples that offer us a glimmer of hope: that elderly couple in the produce section, holding hands as they pick out fresh tomatoes; or your own grandparents, who have been married for fifty years and grin at each other gleefully at their golden-anniversary dinner. The veneer is lovely, as is the standard it sets. But the truth is that we know nothing of the pain they've endured and the sacrifices they've made to get to this place. And yet those moments and people, those "examples" and cultural references, are precisely what fan the flames of our obsession to "become one" with another person. "You complete me," Jerry says to his love interest, Dorothy, in the movie *Jerry Maguire*. Those just might be three of the most dangerous words ever spoken on film.

What if monogamous, romantic marriage is nothing more than a fad gone too far? I liked big '80s hair as much as the next girl, but I didn't want it anymore once it passed its prime. I was fully ready to let it go. What if, collectively, as a culture, we decided that big hair is where it's at, now and for always? You'd wake up in another thirty years and still be perming and teasing and hairspraying. You might eventually start to feel like something that requires so much maintenance cannot be natural, that it might not be the best thing for you. But all around you, people would be looking at you in dismay—even shock—if you attempted a sleek bob, or if you were to wear your hair in braids or a French twist. You'd be a pariah because anything other than big hair simply wouldn't do, no matter how irritating, problematic, and downright bad for your hair its upkeep might have become for countless women. All around you, women might be failing at sustaining this hairstyle, and yet the whole time, people would be telling you that all you should be aspiring to have is perfect big hair.

Although it's impossible to get your hands on any concrete, scientifically sound numbers for several reasons, including the fact that so many people lie about infidelity even in anonymous surveys, it's commonly reported that 40 to 50 percent of marriages end in divorce. Peggy Vaughan, author of *The Monogamy Myth: A Personal Handbook for Dealing with Affairs* and founder of the website DearPeggy. com, explains, "The reality is that monogamy is not the norm, not by today's standards, anyway. *Conservative estimates are that 60 percent of men and 40 percent of women will have an extramarital affair.*"[9] Vaughan also says that the statistics become "even more significant when we consider the total number of marriages involved, since it's unlikely that all the men and women having affairs happen to be married to each other. If even half of the women having affairs (or 20 percent) are married to men not included in the 60 percent having affairs, then at least one partner will have an affair in approximately 80 percent of all marriages."[10] Exact numbers we might not have. But we do have the story those numbers tell, inconsistencies and all. The real "norm," then, as Vaughan herself explains, is infidelity.

In popular culture, we can look to the research and writing of Stephany Alexander, an infidelity and relationship expert, and founder of the website WomanSavers. com, which helps women avoid cheaters and "players" by allowing them to rate and research men. Alexander's site has obviously touched a nerve, presumably because so many people are affected by our nonmonogamous culture. The *New York Times, Wall Street Journal,* CNN, MSNBC, and a rash of other media outlets have covered WomanSavers.com and solicit Alexander's take on the current state of infidelity. In a piece entitled "Cheating and Infidelity Statistics: Are Men Cheating More Than Women?" Alexander writes, "Recent studies reveal that 45–55% of married women and 50–60% of married men engage in extramarital sex at some time or another during their relationship." She explains how "accurate infidelity stats are so difficult to come by because people lie or are embarrassed."[11] Of course. The following is a small sampling of her unscientific but incredibly telling results.

Do you still believe in the institution of marriage?

Yes, strongly. 2,319 votes (66%)

Yes, but only if you plan on having children. 191 votes (5%)

No, I've seen/had enough bad experience to not want to get married. 629 votes (18%)

No, I'd rather just live together. 347 votes (9%)

*   *   *

Have you ever cheated on your man?

Yes. 6433 votes (52%)

No. 5,759 votes (47%)

＊ ＊ ＊

Would you ever cheat?

Yes, if I could get away with it. 1,437 votes (31%)

Yes, but I'd feel guilty. 679 votes (15%)

No, I have too much respect for my partner. 1,361 votes (30%)

No, cheating is immoral. 1,031 votes (22%)

＊ ＊ ＊

Would you forgive your partner if he had a sexual affair?

Yes. 1,088 votes (31%)

No. 2,389 votes (68%)

*   *   *

Has your guy ever cheated on you?

No. 15,653 votes (10%)

Yes, I caught him red-handed. 77,528 votes (54%)

I've suspected, but never caught him. 50,279 votes (35%)[12]

The bottom line is this: We don't know how many people cheat, because studies and statistics and respondents lie. But there is no doubt about the fact that people cheat or want to cheat or think about cheating *all the time.* And men are no longer doing the lion's share of the betraying. The fact that women are catching up to them has a lot to do with the Internet. A surprising number of websites and "dating" services allow married people to seek other married or single people to have affairs with. The Ashley Madison Agency's site proclaims that it's designed for "women seeking romantic affairs—and the men who want to fulfill them." The banner across the top of the homepage reads, "When Monogamy Becomes Monotony." On MarriedSecrets.com, the homepage states, "Studies indicate up to 30% of those people using online dating services are married. Why not join a site specifically designed for you? With MarriedSecrets.

com, there's: no excuses, no explanations . . . just great people waiting to meet you." Then there's LonelyCheatingWives. com, MarriedDateLink.com, and DiscreetAdventures.com, where people can "meet other attached women and men seeking discreet romantic affairs."

All sorts of organizations, conventions, blogs, and newsletters are available for people in open marriages, or swingers, or people who are polyamorous—Polyamory. org, PolyamorySociety.org, Polyweekly.com, and *Loving More* magazine, to name just a few. An entire culture exists out there; it's just that a lot of people don't know—or don't want to know—about it. Many people assume that these communities are full of predators and freaks. Not so. In fact, a number of celebrities—whom American society holds in the same high regard as other cultures do their royalty—allegedly are or have been in open relationships or "arrangements": Mo'Nique and her husband, Sid; George Michael and his partner, Kenny Goss; Ossie Davis and his wife, Ruby Dee; Diana and George Melly; and Simone de Beauvoir and her husband, Jean-Paul Sartre, are just a few of the growing number of people in the public eye who had or have open marriages. Oscar-winning actress Tilda Swinton and her husband, John Byrne, are among the most recent couples to gain media attention for their open relationship. Tilda openly has another lover, Sondro Kopp, outside of their marriage. Notable feminists are also on the list: "Patricia Ireland, a second-waver who was president of the National

Organization for Women from 1991–2001, happily had both a husband and a longtime girlfriend," reveals Jennifer Baumgardner in *Look Both Ways.*[13] It shouldn't come as any surprise that such an empowered woman would see the value in having relationships that fulfilled her in markedly different ways than her experiences with men did.

Alfred Kinsey himself was in an open marriage. He included the following findings in his study:

10 percent of the population is gay;

Sexuality is a spectrum, with the majority of people falling somewhere in between straight and gay, rather than firmly on one side or the other;

Married women, on average, have sex 2.8 times a week;

Approximately 50 percent of all married men are adulterous;

26 percent of females are adulterous by their forties;

12 percent of females and 22 percent of males reported an erotic response to a sadomasochistic story; and

55 percent of females and 50 percent of males reported having responded erotically to being bitten.[14]

Little has changed in the sixty years since Kinsey's findings, although I suppose society has some greater awareness (and perhaps even acceptance and interest) surrounding alternative lifestyles. There is still a vast difference between the societal perceptions and the realities of love, sex, relationships, and marriage. The big question is why, given all we know, is there still such a discrepancy between what we want and what we actually manifest? It seems to stem from the fantasy and romance of the Perfect Man myth, which is still very much alive for girls and women alike. For those for whom monogamy really does work, I say kudos. But I no longer believe it's the norm. History, science, and popular culture point to countless examples that make me wonder who the real minority is.

for three years after I confessed my

relationship with Grace to Christopher, I kept my mouth shut. I never mentioned the affair or my well-formed and ever-expanding fantasies about having another such experience, sans the fallout. I couldn't figure out how to have the sex and the relationship without the lying and the guilt and the hurt. I was so fearful of ruining my marriage that I didn't know what else to do except sit tight. I loved him and our life together. I didn't want to lose him, especially over sex, when we had so much else that was good. We were good partners and parents. Good balances for one another.

But those three years took their toll on me, and while I was living in that dream house in the suburbs and negotiating all of its perilous social constructs (think high school on crack), my ideas were beginning to crystallize. Finally, I got to a point where I was no longer afraid of losing my marriage, because the idea of its continuing in its current state wasn't viable. It felt like a revelation because I finally thought I understood the root of my unhappiness in a relationship in which I "should have" found great happiness.

I decided to write Christopher a long letter and mail it to him. I mailed it right before a long trip I was taking, so I was sure he'd get it while I was away. I wrote about how sad I was that our sex life had all but disappeared. I wrote about the fact that I enjoyed sex too much to go on without it. I wrote that things had to change, that he had to wake up and start seeing me as his sexual partner, seeing me in general, and honoring my needs.

"You're right," he said to me over the phone after reading my letter. "I'm missing everything. I'm missing our daughter, and I'm missing you. I'm just sleepwalking through it all." And things began to change. He started paying attention to his body, exercising, and eating better. He started paying attention to my body, touching me differently, responding to me in the way I wanted and needed him to.

But even with Christopher's newfound alertness, his libido and mine were still divided. He seemed to be able to go without sex entirely, to simply have no need or desire for it. We eventually asked a doctor about our situation, and, after ruling out any medical problems, she said that some people just have no drive, and it's not something that can or necessarily needs to be cured. I, on the other hand, craved sex. And although I had no trouble "gilding the lily" all on my own, I missed sex with a partner or partners.

I had done my due diligence. I had done the research. I had given it the old college try. I had to face the facts. I believed I had four choices: settle for the marriage I had, in the face of all the evidence that such a dynamic is highly unlikely to work; have affairs and deal with all of the stress and risks involved; get divorced and lose out on a perfectly wonderful marriage; or embark on something new altogether. Although the last option was frightening and risky, it was the one I kept coming back to. I figured I had nothing to lose. So, armed with that knowledge, I decided to brave the consequences. I took a deep breath and set off to talk to Christopher about the idea of opening our marriage.

Chapter 5

this is a test

When they talked about it, she realized that she wanted to show him how they could still be together and love each other and be married—even if they slept with other people. Figuring a threesome would be a good place to start, she invited her best friend to sleep with them. The three of them were together for a while, until it turned out that the friend wanted to sleep only with the husband. And so she asked whether she could sleep with other people, too, and her husband said yes—but a few ground rules needed to be laid out. And so their open marriage began.

"you're crazy," Christopher said.

"Why?" I asked.

"I don't want to sleep with other people, and I don't want you to sleep with other people."

We were lying side by side in our bed, and I immediately felt my body stiffen. Instinctively, I pulled away from him. "You don't want me to sleep with other people, or you don't want me to *want* to sleep with other people?"

He paused. "Both."

"But you can't stop me from wanting what I want. What if I want to sleep with women?"

I thought that bringing up the prospect of my sleeping with another woman, or even bringing a woman into our bed, would be the easiest way to broach the subject. I missed sleeping with women, and I thought that if Christopher were included, we might be able to test the waters of this whole open-relationship thing, to figure out if it was going to work for both of us.

"You mean like Grace?" he asked, without missing a beat.

"Yes, *like* Grace. But also, *not* like Grace." Of course, that situation had ended badly, and maybe he had brought it up to be hurtful, but I stopped myself from taking the bait. Instead, I asked, "Weren't things better around here during the six months she and I were sleeping together?

Again, he paused. "Yes," he admitted.

It was a clear opening. I decided that this had to be the moment, and so I told him the things I had been scared to say for three years because I was afraid they would be too hurtful—and because I was afraid that he might leave.

But it was becoming impossible for me to live this way, and I couldn't not talk about it anymore. I wanted him to understand and I wanted, desperately, to be happy. I decided that if telling him the truth meant he would leave, that was a risk I was finally going to have to take. Clinging to a relationship that left me feeling unhappy—because I was afraid I would be unhappy when it was gone—suddenly struck me as beyond ridiculous.

I delicately explained to Christopher that I'd felt happy and satisfied when I was seeing Grace, because I finally wasn't looking to him to fulfill something that he either couldn't or didn't want to give me. I told him that it had felt like a relief because it alleviated the pressure on him and on me. Because of my relationship with Grace, I was able to be with him without feeling guilty about my needs or resentful about not having them met.

He told me that the sex with Grace hadn't bothered him as much as my lying about it. I knew this already. It wasn't the first time we'd discussed it. This foray into open marriage was no short jaunt, after all; it was a long haul getting from point A to point B, from closed to open. And it inevitably involved rehashing a lot of conversations again and again. But bit by bit, we were reaching a point where it seemed like we both might be interested in giving it a whirl, at least to see how it would feel. The idea of living openly—and of naming and embracing that choice, rather than keeping it tucked under the stairs like the ugly stepchild—increasingly seemed a necessity for our relationship. We agreed, with time, that the *idea* of open marriage did make sense. I was already there, but I knew it would work only if Christopher actually bought into it, too. I wasn't interested in trying to maintain something he wasn't onboard with. I realized that we might very well still end up separating, because talking and agreeing about it didn't mean that an open marriage was going to be functional in practice. Still, I was as prepared as anyone can be to try something that had just as good a chance of saving a marriage as it did of destroying it.

After our plethora of conversations, the time had finally come to stop talking and start doing. "So, what do you think?" I asked one night. "How would you feel about actually opening our marriage?" Christopher gave me a knowing look. He wasn't surprised that I'd brought it up again.

"Even though we're doing better now," I told him. And we were. Sex had become more regular, but it wasn't enough, and I knew it wasn't ever going to be.

I knew Christopher was about to ask me again how it would work: Would it just be women? Would it be men, too? Would they come to our house?

We'd been over this a thousand times; was he just testing me at this point? Was he simply trying to get me to admit that I wanted to sleep with other men? I wasn't sure. But I knew, regardless, that this was a process, and that its logical first step was for the two of us to be with a woman together. Then we could see where that led us.

Christopher apologized for not being enough for me, as he often did, but I didn't need to hear that. Being sexually incompatible is no one's fault, but that doesn't make it any less of an issue. We both agreed that we would allow no strangers in the house, as we were equally invested in protecting Emily and prioritizing our family. I had someone in mind, though, who was not a stranger, someone Emily knew and felt comfortable with already. And if she happened to spend the night one night, it wouldn't make Emily suspicious in the slightest.

"What do you think about my friend from book club, Lisbeth?" I asked casually. "Haven't you ever thought about sleeping with her?"

"No," he said. Then his face softened. "Okay, yes, but . . . "

Lisbeth had come up before. She hung out at our house a lot, and she and Christopher were rather flirty on occasion. Still, whenever I asked him about actually doing something about it, he'd always say the same things: "She'd never want to sleep with me"; "She's fifteen years younger than I am"; and "I don't need to be with anyone else." I believed that last part. I have always known that I'm enough for Christopher, which is part of what made opening our relationship so difficult. I've always felt like it would have been an easier conversation if his libido had been on par with mine.

"But I'm definitely attracted to her," he added. Yeah. I was too. She was gorgeous, with thick blond hair and an athlete's trim body. And this particular night, Christopher changed his tune. Perhaps he realized that our testing these waters was inevitable, so why not with Lisbeth? "If you think you can make that happen, bring it on," he said. I shook my head and teased him about how unattractive frat-speak was coming from a grown man, and voilà, we were off on another subject.

I already knew Lisbeth was interested; we'd talked about the three of us sleeping together plenty of times. So it wasn't a matter of whether or not I could "bring it on." It was more a question of how things were going to go if we actually went through with it. It was impossible not to ponder the reality of what had thus far been a fantasy—especially because if we did it, and it went well, we would actually be in an open marriage.

Christopher had asked me on a number of occasions what being in an open marriage might really *mean*. "I'm talking about in the broadest sense here," he said. "What is an open marriage?" I'd had to admit to him that I didn't really know. All I had to go on was what I'd read about, and the more I read, the more I realized how many different forms it can take, and how it means different things to different couples. Some consider it "swinging"; for others, it's a conscious choice—what people call a "lifestyle." For me, those concepts were different because one involved partner swapping and the other meant having open relationships outside of a marriage, and I wasn't looking for the former. Others see open marriage as another way of "doing" polyamory, which resonated with me, even though, at that early stage, I was definitely focusing on sexual fulfillment. But I wasn't so naive as to imagine that love wouldn't at least someday, and in some ways, play into our experiences; the idea seemed scary, but also like it wouldn't be an unpleasant by-product of an open marriage.

A man who calls himself Alan maintains a blog called Polyamorous Percolations. His definition of open marriage is "when members of a married, life-committed couple take secondary lovers, together and/or separately." He describes it as one of the most common forms of polyamory. The key to its success, Alan maintains, is that "everyone knows and approves of the whole interrelationship." Furthermore, he says, it's important that everyone involved in such a scenario "realizes that they are all involved with each other, and all respect and honor each other's needs, boundaries, and well-being."[1]

When it comes to information on this subject, there isn't a heck of a lot out there. But, in doing my research, I found this site particularly helpful in defining what I was looking for in my open marriage. Such relationships appear to include every possible variation and permutation—from people whose secondary partners live with them to those who never have "second contact" with their liaisons (essentially, they only have one-night stands). Some see certain lovers on certain occasions, ranging dramatically from once a week to once a year. Some people require that emotions play a significant part in their outside relationships, and others insist specifically that they don't. "Open marriage" is a catchall, and not a perfect one, to say the least. But it's the terminology we choose because it covers the flexibility and changeability that its participants are searching for. Just like a traditional marriage, an open marriage is not a sure bet: It's a constantly evolving thing, and we still don't know how the phases of our marriage will look as our life together unfolds.

I was hugely relieved to discover the existence of this world, this entire network of people who are out there defining marriage for themselves. "They've looked at the traditional cycle of dating-cheating-marrying-and-divorcing and thought, that just makes no sense to me," writes Michelle Chihara for Nerve.com.[2] Given the current state of marriage and fidelity, Chihara maintains that it's hard to argue against overhauling the system. The polyamorists she spoke to for her piece are interested in "writing their own rules" for their relationships because "marriage is just one more area of life where [young people] don't trust received wisdom."[3] It's an ideal approach, again, as long as all parties are onboard. Polyamorists refuse to take marriage at face value, and instead accept only what *actually* works, rather than what's *supposed* to work.

the possibility of emotional involvement

or attachment was the primary thing that scared Christopher when we were getting started.

"Are you going to fall in love with someone else?" he asked me.

"I don't know, but it won't be sex that'll make me fall in love," I told him. "In fact, I'm betting that sleeping with people takes the mystery out of the equation. It might even ensure that I never mistake lust or infatuation with falling in love."

Now that I'm as far as I am into my open marriage, that's turned out to be a rather prophetic statement. I have had relationships in which I've developed deep emotions, but only in one have I felt able to say I am "in love," and that's with my current girlfriend, Jemma. Others have been nothing more than casual friends; still others I've loved. But for me, falling in love with someone is precious and rare. My being in love with Jemma doesn't compromise my being in love with Christopher; the feelings complement each other because they broaden and strengthen my capacity to love. Love begets love; it does not cancel out its predecessors.

Other things scared Christopher, too. He had a hard time agreeing with me that sex and love are not always inextricable, and that loving other people wouldn't mean that we wouldn't still love each other. I needed him to be completely comfortable before we moved forward, but I also realized that, no matter what, I was still persuading him. He wouldn't ever have been interested in open marriage if I hadn't been the driving force behind the idea. He seemed to need to garner some sort of "proof"—an experience that would jar him out of what I considered to be his unfounded convictions. I think he was scared that I might leave him, or that I might decide I was a lesbian. I think he was scared that he would realize that *he* didn't want *me* anymore, either, because he'd find someone he liked more, or because he wouldn't be able to free himself from the image of me with someone else.

I understood that the idea of opening up our marriage brought up all kinds of fears for him (it did for me, too), but I have to admit that I was blown away that Christopher didn't leap at the opportunity to invite another woman into our bed. As far as I can tell, there aren't many husbands or boyfriends who wouldn't love the idea of their wife or girlfriend opening the door to the bedroom and saying, "Honey, I want you to meet Ginger." But not my husband. He doesn't like strip clubs. He enjoys sex within the confines of a relationship. I know, I know—most women would consider me the winner of the loyalty lotto, and I'm sure plenty of people are shaking their heads in amazement that the two of us ended up together. But together we are. There's a lot to be said for opposites attracting. It creates a surprising balance where there might otherwise be a difficult volatility.

i'd had my fill of the late-night "what if?" conversations, Christopher had agreed to give it a go with Lisbeth, and I was ready to approach her about it. Even though she and I had discussed it several times, our

conversations mostly involved innuendo. We teased each other about her wanting to attack my husband, and about the two of us sleeping together someday. I have no clue whether she thought it would ever really happen. But the lengthy buildup seemed to speak for itself. I was simply waiting for the time to be just right. I'm a big believer in destiny, and, as my spiritual advisor, Jimmy Belasco (whom I meet with biweekly for a dose of palatable Taoist advice to help me on my path), consistently reminds me, "Everything happens as it's supposed to." When you open yourself to the universe and all of its possibilities, you will find what you are seeking, and what you are intended to find. Thus, my friendship with Lisbeth was serendipitous.

I was attracted to Lisbeth from the very first day we met. Aside from her beautiful hair and amazing body, she was wickedly funny and incredibly smart. We met at book club, a group made up of twenty- and thirtysomethings, some married, some single, some with children and some without. These women were the exact opposite of the ones in my planned community. They were politically liberal, for the most part. Interestingly, though, we discovered after just a few book club meetings that they all seemed to be onboard the Disney monorail of monogamous marriage, 2.5 kids, and a dog named Sparky.

The book that shed light on this fact was *Written on the Body,* by Jeanette Winterson, about an incredible, life-altering affair that the central character has with a married woman.

Though the author never reveals the protagonist's gender, the sensuality and emotion in the relationship are raw, intense, and wholly female. Shockingly, our entire group concurred that the central character was a man—everyone except for Lisbeth and me, that is.

Our shared interpretation of *Written on the Body* was just the starting point of what would become an amazingly strong friendship. After that night at book club, I asked her to have dinner with me one night, and then drinks another, and before we knew it, we were hanging out all the time. We'd go to bars and concerts. She'd come over and spend time with my family. Sometimes she'd baby-sit so Christopher and I could have a night out. Lisbeth and Emily adored each other; in fact, I'm pretty sure Emily thought Lisbeth was *her* best friend, not mine.

Lisbeth and I were incredibly like-minded, especially about sex and relationships. In other ways, we were quite different. She was single and ten years younger than I, and had grown up in a conservative Catholic family. Before meeting her, I spent months, prior to initiating the idea of open marriage with my husband, feeling like I was some sort of freak, like my libido was out of control, like I was selfish—a bad wife and a bad mother. But being with her and talking to her seemed to legitimize my emerging feelings about sexuality and marriage, convince me that the questions and doubts I had weren't particular to me, and confirm for me that open marriage wasn't appealing only to people who are married, or who are getting older and feeling dissatisfied in their relationships.

I'd been consumed by the idea that I was interested in having relationships outside my marriage only because I'd gotten stuck in my routine, or because I was going through some sort of early midlife crisis, or because something was wrong with me. But here was Lisbeth—this beautiful, young, single woman—who felt the same way I did. I often shared with her how I was feeling about the lack of sex in my marriage. I confessed that I thought about divorcing Christopher. I talked through my confusion with her, asking her time and again how it could be that things were simultaneously so good and so bad.

"People are not built for monogamy," she said to me early on. We were talking about my feeling guilty for wanting to sleep with other people. Lisbeth saw no need for guilt; she got that I would want to stay in my marriage *and* be with other people. "So what's the big deal?" she continued. "Sex feels good. When did sex and love become so inseparable?"

"I don't know," I said, shaking my head.

"I'll tell you what it is—the Church," she said. "It's gotta be the Church. They don't like anything that feels or tastes or sounds or looks good."

"Tastes? Really?"

"Have you taken Communion lately?"

"I don't think you should let the media off the hook so easily," I countered. "Movies about perfect princesses and TV shows about flawless families certainly aren't helping matters."

"Well, whatever it is, it sucks," she concluded.

A happy sexual tension existed between us. We were joyful about being friends. I was hot for her, yes, but I was trying my best to work on my marriage and be honest with Christopher. In the back of my mind, I admit, I did imagine that the three of us would sleep together one day, but I still had plenty of thoughts and feelings and desires to work out before that could ever happen. Even though Lisbeth had expressed interest, I didn't want to lose her as a friend. There were times when people had mistaken us for girlfriends, given the palpable intimacy between us. She never denied it, and we relished the times we got to snuggle up on the sofa, playing with each other's hair. We were both very comfortable in this semisexual space.

Once it seemed inevitable that Christopher and I would open up our marriage, I decided it was time to seriously broach the topic with Lisbeth. She was almost as flirty with Christopher as she was with me, and when I mentioned the idea of the three of us sleeping together—for real—she was intrigued. We shared our fears and desires about what a threesome would be like. She all but lived with us as it was, and we all adored one another—the physical act of sex was really the only thing missing from the equation. We discussed the fact that a lot of people would consider our dynamic socially deviant, but there were plenty of things about our shared thinking that went against the grain. I was as honest as I could be, admitting that, as interested as I was in moving forward, I was also scared: scared of losing my best friend, scared of losing my husband. In my mind, the script was already rolling: *Kelly thought it would be fun to invite her best friend, Susan, into their bed,* the voice-over would say, *but Kelly never imagined she'd lose them both . . . to each other.*

TV movies and blindly accepted social conventions aside, Lisbeth and I agreed that we both wanted to give it a shot. We didn't have a plan; we just figured that when the time was right, we'd know it. Sure enough, just a few weeks later, all of the planets seemed to align.

"Let's do it tonight," I said to her. We were at my house, watching a DVD on the couch. It was a perfect night. Emily was staying over at a friend's, and Christopher was due back from a meeting within a few hours. She smiled and gave me a knowing look.

"You sure?" she asked.

"Are you?" I asked back.

"Yeah," she said. "I am. As long as you are."

When Christopher came home, he slid onto the couch next to me, putting his hand on my thigh. Lisbeth's hand was already on my other leg, and within moments, the sexual tension in the room was palpable. It wasn't but a few seconds before I felt their hands touch under the throw. I watched as they caught each other's eyes. Christopher's face didn't betray a thing, but I knew he knew.

"I'm beat," he said a short while later. "I'm going to bed."

"We'll be up after the movie," I said. He kissed me and headed for the stairs.

"What about me?" Lisbeth asked. He looked at me first—as if for my permission. I smiled and raised my eyebrows, implying, *It's your call.* He walked over to her and kissed her long and hard.

Laughing, he shook his head. "You girls." Lisbeth and I finished watching our movie before following Christopher upstairs. We slipped into bed on either side of him, as if that were what we'd always done. And everything that followed that night felt equally natural.

I couldn't keep from smiling as I watched my husband run his hands over Lisbeth's breasts and down her hips. He looked awed, as if this were the first time he had ever touched a woman like that—not just her, but any woman. It was amazing to watch them together. It was hot, but it was also sweet. She was lost in him, and he in her. I was able to see Christopher as a human being for the first time in years—not as my husband or my daughter's father, but as a man, a sexual being, a person who needed to be wanted. Lisbeth was bossy and aggressive with him, and he listened to her unfailingly. She was also tender, and it made my heart happy to see him so enthralled.

Later, he shared with me that watching Lisbeth and me together was an incredible experience for him as well. She showed him how to give me a G-spot orgasm, a feat that he'd never managed. It sounds strange, I know, but it was also delightful, even charming, and exactly what I'd been craving. The three of us were the same in bed together as we were outside of it—we talked and joked and played. Before the sun came up, Lisbeth made her way back to the guest room so that she'd be there if Emily got home early.

That morning, Christopher cooked, Lisbeth watched cartoons with Emily, and I marveled at how everything and nothing had changed. After Lisbeth left, Christopher plopped down next to me on the couch, shaking his head. "Wow," he said with a laugh.

"I know," I replied. "Wow."

"You okay?"

"Yeah. You?"

"Uh-huh. Wow." We talked about how much fun, how hot, and how surprisingly natural the experience had been. Christopher confessed to having been terribly nervous, but so turned on when the two of us crawled into bed with him that he figured, *What the hell?* He told me how much he loved me, and how I constantly amazed him. "I never would have been brave enough to do something like this without your prompting," he said. "Thank you."

I was happy and relieved and amazed. Sure, it had been only one night, but it had also been one incredibly normal morning. We were all on the same page. We all felt that what we were doing was perfectly fine because we all felt comfortable—with ourselves and with each other. I felt like screaming, "See!" at the top of my lungs, but I knew that wasn't necessary. Getting to this point of comfort and readiness hadn't been easy, but it had been worth the wait. And so I simply breathed a sigh of relief and smiled as I thought about what this might mean for our marriage's future. More than ever, open marriage seemed like the ultimate expression of trust in both myself and my husband.

during the next six months, Christopher and I had many conversations about how happy we were, and how well this supposedly "crazy" idea was working out. We realized that we had been living within a convention that simply did not jibe with who we were, individually and together, as human beings. We had fallen in love and gotten married because that was what we were supposed to do, not because we had thought carefully about the lifestyle that would best suit us. We marveled at how nice it was having Lisbeth around: someone else to cook with and clean with; someone else to play with Emily; someone else to love. It was incredible how loving Lisbeth made us love each other more. We had all cared about one another before we began sleeping together, after all, so the sex became simply another component of our relationship.

Throughout our time with Lisbeth, Christopher and I marveled at how content we felt. He admitted that I had been right, and he was thrilled. He loved watching Lisbeth and me together, and loved it when I watched the two of them as well.

"She's so hot," he would say to me. "Not that you're not; it's just . . . she's hot. She's young and she wants me and it's different and nice when we're all together. And the sex is great." These comments were like epiphanies. They didn't make me jealous—I cannot emphasize that enough. I like it when I see my husband happy, and that extends to seeing another person loving him. And, as an added bonus, it's a turn-on. Seeing someone else so enjoying him reminds me of why I enjoy him, too. I felt like his attraction to Lisbeth was also working to align our sex drives, even though I knew that his libido was likely to eventually wane again. That was the nature of the beast, and of Christopher.

One of Christopher's friends recently told us that we are the most evolved couple he knows. And that was exactly how I was feeling as we were embarking upon this new journey. We weren't ashamed of our wants and needs, we delighted in each other's happiness, and we were honest with each other through it all. We were finally managing to be true to ourselves and each other, even if doing so flew in the face of conventional images of marriage.

"What if you really do have it all figured out?" Christopher's friend asked us that day.

"I don't know about that," Christopher responded, "but I do know that having sex with other people—heck, *loving* other people—isn't going to be our downfall."

Christopher finally got it. He simply couldn't argue with his own happiness or mine. Initially, he had said that he understood open marriage, but only in theory. But starting down this loving, honest path with Lisbeth was exactly what Christopher needed to embrace the lifestyle in practice.

After the three of us had been together for several months, my husband continued to sleep with Lisbeth, but I didn't. It was her choice, not mine. But I respected her interests (or lack thereof). I didn't mind that Christopher was sleeping with her. It made him happy. How could it not have? She was like the ultimate fantasy fulfillment for him. I missed having sex with her, but it was important to me that she was honest about how she was feeling. As it turned out, she "just wasn't that into" me, as the saying goes. And nothing is less sexy than disinterest.

My husband's sexual relationship with Lisbeth ended when she met a guy whom she wanted to be with exclusively. After it was over, Christopher and I had to reassess where we were. We had to rethink—or create, really—the "rules." I confessed that I might want to sleep with other men, which came as no surprise to him. And Christopher admitted that one of his biggest concerns about that was that he'd walk into a restaurant one night and hear one guy say to another, "I fucked that guy's wife."

"I would feel so stupid and small," Christopher told me, "as if I couldn't satisfy you myself, and so you had to look somewhere else." The funny thing is, my reaction would be quite the opposite. If the situation were reversed, I wouldn't be able to resist feeling a little smug, smiling at the woman who had said those words and thinking to myself, *He's amazing, isn't he?*

Because Christopher and I were coming from such different places, though, it was crucial that we figure out how to "do" open marriage, which, truth be told, is something we are still trying to discover now, three years into our field research.

Our whole process has been about redefining terms and renegotiating parameters, and that changes every time one of us meets someone new, or anytime one of us wants to discuss something we haven't tried before. An open marriage is a scary proposition. It calls into question nearly everything we think we know and accept about sexuality, sensuality, and marriage. But there are plenty of compelling reasons why it works for Christopher and me, and why it was worth taking a shot at revolutionizing our union. My sexual rights are just as important to me as any number of my other civil rights. I have no interest in taking away my friends' husbands, or converting people to the idea that open marriage is a better option, but I just know this for myself: I need more.

For those of us who feel that way, three challenges lie along the road to rectifying our situation: We must disentangle sex and love; we must consciously engage our own sensuality and longing for touch; and we must let go of our fears of being unaccepted or alone. I continue to be intrigued by the question of how we might live if we followed our desires. And that is what open marriage allows us to explore.

Chapter 6

having our cake
and eating it, too

Figuring it all out took a lot of talking, but the couple was happy. She experimented here and there when she was out of town. She slept with other people and felt more connected to her husband. She slowly began to accept that she was okay, that her choices were right for her, and that her husband was onboard. And that was all that mattered.

in the months after our relationship with Lisbeth ended, as we began laying out some ground rules for our burgeoning new lifestyle, I realized that I didn't want to wait months or years for another Lisbeth to come along—and who knew if we could even find someone else like her? I sure didn't want to go back to the way things had been before, either. I wanted to have other partners. I wanted to "date," for lack of a better word. I wasn't just looking for a warm body. I was looking for someone smart and funny and, yes, attractive. I was looking for someone who could slip into the role of "insta-boyfriend" (or girlfriend), with whom I could spend a night (or several) and have great sex, yes, but also connect intellectually or emotionally. I didn't leap into the relative unknown of open marriage just so I could have a one-night stand with some drunk guy. Hell, I could hire someone if I wanted that—and it'd be easier, and likely safer. No, I like to be courted, if only for one night. I get turned on by connecting. I get turned on by being seen.

In *Against Love,* Laura Kipnis explains this concept beautifully: "The new beloved mirrors this fascinating new self back to you, and admit it, you're madly in love with both of them."[1] There's no question that falling in love has a lot to do with seeing what the other person sees in you, and loving yourself more because of it. I'm not ashamed of wanting to see my best self mirrored back to me. I like how I look in a lover's eyes. And no matter what, how a new lover perceives us is invariably different from the way we appear to someone who's loved us for years, and who's seen us through all of the ups and downs of a long-term relationship. Both visions can be equally amazing. When I see the way a new lover looks at me, it reminds me why my husband fell in love with me and why I fell in love with him. It makes me aware that I'm still that person, and that understanding can reinvigorate our relationship and help me value what we have.

As you can imagine, what I'm looking for is not easy to find. I am open, not promiscuous. I am not simply looking for more of everything; I am looking for specific things: positive, happy experiences; something that will complement, rather than compete with, my marriage. In *The Ethical Slut,* the bible of many polyamorists, authors Dossie Easton and Catherine A. Liszt write, "One-night stands can be intense, life-enhancing, and fulfilling; so can lifetime love affairs."[2] The fact that it's possible to have both types of relationships may seem contradictory, but in fact they're remarkably compatible. I have found great joy and satisfaction in both. It's only our own social baggage that tells us that the two must be mutually exclusive.

One criticism I've heard time and time again from people who oppose open marriage is that it seems like a selfish free-for-all. In the aftermath of writing my article "Portrait of a Marriage" for *Tango* magazine, I marveled at the comments people posted about my piece, which, interestingly, they were still making more than a year and a half after it was published. Here's one example of a fairly typical remark: "I think it's sad—she wants her cake & to eat it too. We'd all love to have sex 24/7, but the realities of life and the realities of relationships don't always permit it. Grow up."[3] The writer implies that an open marriage is a self-indulgent copout somehow, an easy way to deal with a relationship that is failing or lacking. But nothing could be further from the truth. Open marriage is not easy. It would have been easier for me to remain unhappy in my closed marriage, actually, but I just couldn't do it. I have every right to my own happiness, but I've had to fight for it; even coming around to believing that I have that right has been difficult.

I think some critics of open marriage are put off by the idea that a woman might consider happiness her right, especially if it's happiness gained at the *perceived* expense of a husband or family. But isn't my being happy in my day-to-day life and living honestly *better* for my family? Emily, for one, is as happy as can be. We haven't told her that anything has changed and, as a result, nothing *has* changed in her eyes. Christopher and I love each other and we're together, parenting and loving her. What we do in private is not her concern, just as the private lives of parents in a closed marriage are none of the children's concern. Kids don't need to know, shouldn't know, about their parents' sex lives.

The types of comments I received from *Tango's* readers often reminded me of the schoolyard banter of my childhood. "Jane's using two colors of Play-Doh!" "Allen ate a second cookie!" Jane and Allen weren't bothering anyone else with their behavior, but the tattletales among us—whether they're elementary schoolers or mature adults with kids of their own—just can't stand by and allow others to enjoy what they wouldn't dare to do themselves. A relatively common law of human behavior seems to be: If I have to follow the rules, then you do, too. It didn't make any sense to me then, and it certainly doesn't make any sense to me now. It begs the question: Who has some serious growing up to do?

In many situations, when the subject of my marriage arises, I find myself defending open marriage and defining what it is for us—and more frequently what it isn't. The perception is somehow that those of us in open relationships walk into a room and say, "Come and get it." People are quick to classify it as anything but healthy. But it's been abundantly clear in my conversations with people that, all too often, they're projecting their own insecurities onto me because they see my behavior as threatening to their ways of thinking or living. Why should I pose such a threat? Is it due to a lack of trust among partners? The fear that I might sleep with their husbands or wives, leaving them out of the loop and out of control? Or is it perhaps that a transference of sorts occurs when they read about the choices I have made? I remind them of their own discontent, and so they lash out at me as a stand-in for their own sexual fears and disappointments, or otherwise painful experiences. One respondent to my article (this time after it was reprinted on HuffingtonPost. com) wrote, "[T]his article to me sounds like a classic case of sexual addiction. The author sounds like a sex-addict."[4] Interestingly, the person admits that their mother's second marriage was to a sex addict. Talk about projection.

I've spoken of my high libido, and it's true that I do enjoy sex very much. But I am not a sex addict. In his book *Contrary to Love,* Dr. Patrick Carnes, an expert in the field of sexual disorders, defines a sex addict as someone who experiences little pleasure, often feels despair in the middle of sex, lives a secret life surrounded by a web of lies, can't control their sexual behavior, has delusional thought patterns and reality distortion.[5] Carnes explains that a sex addict does, or fantasizes about doing, things that he or she doesn't even like. This person may also prioritize sex—in thought and action—above *all* else.

Annie Sprinkle, a sexpert, writer, artist, and performer, who has often been called a sex addict as well, has posted responses to this accusation on her website. She goes through a series of questions often used to "diagnose" the problem, and points mainly to the fact that many of the behaviors associated with sexual addiction aren't necessarily negative in the first place. Sprinkle writes that the diagnosis itself "often makes a disease out of what is often quite reasonable sexual behavior. It emphasizes negative aspects of sex. . . . It can make people feel badly if they simply have an active and varied sex life. Sex addiction can be used as a way to put down socially disapproved of behavior."[6] In other words, the label is often used as a weapon by people who take issue with other people's sexual behavior and preferences. (And, just as an aside, sexual addiction is not considered a disorder in *The Diagnostic and Statistical Manual of Mental Disorders [DSM],* a hefty volume published by the American Psychiatric Association.)

Another commentator, who went by only the name Doc, posted: "Implicitly selfish!!! Either get in or get out . . . and ice yourself down once in a while. . . . "[7] I had to laugh aloud as I imagined Doc taking his or her own frequent cold showers. Although Doc didn't provide any personal information, I couldn't help but wonder if s/he was in a sexless marriage, as the people who respond most negatively to my choices tend to be those who appear to adhere to the "If I'm going to be unhappy, then you have to be unhappy, too" motto.

One poster, who calls himself Anonymous Coward, responded at length to "Portrait of a Marriage" on the *Tango* magazine site. He is an open relationship himself, and speaks to the above point with great precision. "I read through these comments, and I see mostly hatred, shame, and guilt from the 'happily monogamous' crowd, and mostly sharing, loving, and life from the 'you go girl' crowd."[8] Time and again, the people who judge me for my sexual choices—choices that my husband and I are making together as consenting adults—are those who are lacking something in their own lives, who have deviant sexual desires they're stifling, or who are so committed to the social constructs they've been raised on that they simply cannot comprehend or tolerate anything that exists outside of those margins.

Another downside of being out and willing to talk about open marriage is that I get solicited too often, always by men who are sadly misinformed about what being in an open marriage actually means. For starters, it doesn't mean that I have no standards or preferences about the type of person I'd be interested in going out with. I fill people in on my marriage status because it's my reality. But that doesn't make me any less picky than I would have been if Christopher and I had gotten divorced and I had returned to the dating circuit. I'm not interested in casual encounters, which I could find very easily on Craigslist or in any number of other virtual "locations," let alone real ones, if I wanted to. Turns out I have pretty strict standards.

I don't sleep with anyone who's attached unless they, too, are in an open relationship, and I don't sleep with anyone I don't feel a connection with or am not attracted to. I always tell partners—even potential partners—that I'm married. As many things as I do want, there are as many, or more, things I don't want. My whole reason for wanting to have an open marriage is to be with people who are right for me under the right circumstances. So no, I tell naysayers, my bedroom doors are not open to just anyone. Not by a long shot.

after being with Lisbeth, Christopher

and I talked a lot about the boundaries of our new arrangement. I was excited to test the waters, but I was also very clear about my standards, and about wanting that connection, which is key for me. I remember specifically talking with my friend April around this time, about various conferences we'd both attended over the years. As I tried to recall one in particular, she said, "You know—that was the year I had cake and I couldn't even give it away." She was speaking literally—she'd taken a cake to attract people to her booth, and yet not a soul had come to partake. I started laughing. It was the perfect metaphor for how I was feeling in this strange new territory of being married but "allowed" to have other lovers. I had the cake, all right, but not a viable taker in sight. I didn't know where to start, and when I finally did start looking, I came up empty-handed more often than not.

Looking to meet people as a woman in an open marriage is markedly different from what I experienced as a single woman. The most important piece of the puzzle now is that I'm not looking for someone to marry. You'd think this would be a nonissue—that people would be thrilled to date someone who's not available. But my unavailability and the reasoning behind it bring up their own set of challenges to people's preconceived notions of what's "okay." I would actually argue that people find it more acceptable to wind up in a relationship with a married person "by accident"— even though that would fall into the category of cheating— than beginning one in which both parties are okay with the openness of the situation. The straightforwardness of open marriage makes a lot of people uncomfortable, and it takes a very specific type of person to truly understand the fact that a couple might choose open marriage and be happy with it.

My particular circumstances make finding prospects both easier and harder. It's easier because it puts fewer constraints on me. It's harder because I have to really examine what I'm looking for. Basically, I'm free to just be into certain people without having to worry about whether they have a steady job, or what kind of parent they might make. That's a relief on a lot of levels, but it can also take some real mental maneuvering to enjoy the moment while still recognizing and validating the relationship for what it is—or could be.

Being in an open marriage involves a different type of courting. It's a very strange dance. My disclosure about my marriage is always in the back of my mind. I know that I'm presumed to be single, and that I put out a "single" vibe when I'm out, particularly at a party or in other social settings. I do want to meet people, after all. But divulge this information too soon, and I seem to be implying that something's going to happen between the person I'm talking to and me. Say it too late, and it seems like I'm hiding it. Not to mention that saying it at all can be risky: Plenty of times, someone has concluded automatically that I'm a slut. I don't see myself that way, though I will admit to having used the word loosely to describe my sexual prowess—much like women will call themselves or their friends "bitches" in a way that's meant to be affectionate, rather than derogatory. And once people get to know me and understand my life, they don't think of me as a slut, either. But I understand that some, upon first hearing about my relationship and my sexual appetite, imagine I'd sleep with anyone with a pulse at any time.

The most common reaction I get from people who meet me face to face is one of simple curiosity. And though I've positioned myself to some degree as the person who wants to talk about this topic at every turn, the reality is that the questions can be exhausting—just like it's tiring to get asked where you're from after several weeks of being far from home. It can wear a girl down to field the same questions every time she reveals that she's in an open marriage. "Oh my god, really?" "How does that work?" "Your husband lets you sleep with other guys? No way." There are many times when it would be a heck of a lot easier to keep my situation to myself. But that would completely fly in the face of the very thing that makes this work—honesty.

Honestly is especially important when I'm potentially interested in pursuing someone. I do not want to fail to tell someone my deal and end up with a very pissed-off person on my hands, who feels duped once they eventually do find out. But even in my day-to-day life, I've made telling people about my situation a priority, if and when it's appropriate, that is. Anyone who's going to get to know me, as a friend, as a colleague, is going to find out eventually that I'm in an open relationship. I expect people to be forthcoming with me, too, and so oftentimes my revelation can be an icebreaker of sorts. In some cases, it's actually resulted in deeper friendships. I'm a natural confidant because I'm not judgmental. I've been through way too much to criticize what other people have going on in their lives.

However, being the poster child for open marriage is a full-time job, and as much as I enjoy talking about all things body and soul, sometimes I would rather talk about something else. It's that simple. Above all, I am learning how to find balance, and this whole experience has been about processing and talking through my own feelings about what I'm doing. And the encounters I've had that work have been with people who can accept my situation and embrace our dynamic for what it is without minimizing it.

my first experience after Lisbeth

happened when I met Kyle. I was attending a writers' conference on the Jersey shore, and I'd had a long first day of readings and meeting with agents. I decided I needed a break, and snuck out of the hotel before any of the other aspiring authors could glom on to me; I headed down the boardwalk to a local bar to have a moment to myself and enjoy a drink.

The second I walked in, though, I had the overwhelming urge to run back to the sterile hotel bar that I had summarily dismissed. The place was full of hot twentysomethings talking and laughing and drinking. Hip-hop was blaring. I generally think of myself as a relatively attractive person, and am not often rattled by my age, but seeing all of those incredibly good-looking young people that night left me feeling out of my element, to say the least. The day's activities had also contributed to my disorientation: I had been surrounded by many writers in their early twenties, who were vying for the same agents and editors and had resumes far stronger than my own.

I decided not to turn back, though. One drink wasn't going to kill me, and maybe there'd be some material to drum up in this den of iniquity. I drank my first cocktail a little too quickly. I was already nearly exhausted from vacillating between attempting to look as if I were perfectly comfortable sitting alone, and trying to appear as if I were patiently awaiting the arrival of my now very late companion. But halfway into my second drink, I was done faking it.

"I'm too old for this place," I said aloud to no one in particular.

"You're not too old," a voice behind me said. I turned around on my barstool to find a guy who looked like he had been extracted straight from the pages of a J.Crew catalog. He had brown hair and blue eyes, and was six feet tall, with a build that you could tell, even through his clothes, would look damn good without those clothes. I smiled.

"Your mother raised you very well. Thank you," I said.

"Kyle," he said, offering me his hand.

We exchanged the typical pleasantries about work, and then moved on to discussing the crowd. I mentioned feeling a bit out of my league, and Kyle told me he was none too impressed by the girls there.

"They all look the same," he said. "They look like they haven't eaten for weeks because they don't serve food at the tanning salon or the makeup counter." Who knows if he was trying to flatter me, but it was working. He worked in industrial sales. He was twenty-five, intelligent, and very cute. An hour later, when the bar closed, Kyle walked me out.

He invited me to join him and his friends at their next destination, but I declined, offering an early morning ahead of me as my excuse.

"Can I take you out tomorrow night?" he asked. I smiled, thinking there wasn't a chance in hell this guy would call. But why not? I gave him my last name and told him where I was staying.

When I got back to my room the next afternoon after the conference, there was a message waiting for me. It was from Kyle. I paused for a moment. Did I really want to follow through on this? Could he possibly be as cute or as funny as I remembered? What if it was the alcohol or the dark bar? He had been fun to flirt with, but why mess with it? But even as I was thinking these things, I was lifting the receiver to call him.

He met me in my hotel lobby that same night. He walked me out to his car, a small black Mercedes, and opened the passenger-side door for me. He got into the car and put the keys in the ignition, but before he started the engine. he turned to me and asked, "Are you married?"

"I am," I answered.

"Yeah, my friend said he thought you were wearing a wedding ring," he said calmly.

I took a deep breath and apologized for the amount of information I was about to regale him with. I told him that I was in an open marriage. I explained our circumstances: "We don't bring people home. We're not promiscuous. And we have no interest in leaving each other for someone else." I felt relieved even as I was talking. I felt committed to my promise to be honest to potential partners, to Christopher, and to myself.

He looked a little stunned and I asked him if he wanted me to go. "I would completely understand," I said. "It's a lot of information, but I want you to know that I would have told you before anything happened. I mean . . . if it seemed like something might happen." He smiled and started the car.

Later that night, we continued to talk about my marriage and how it worked. Kyle asked lots of questions. And then he surprised me: "Your husband must be amazing," he said.

It was not the typical response—which I'm much more aware of now than I could have been then. And I so appreciated Kyle's understanding. I remember one guy in particular, an aspiring rock star, who told me point blank, "I couldn't be that guy. Even if your husband's down with it, it's not right." The funny thing was, he had a girlfriend but he was obviously ready to take me home. So again, this crazy mix of people's own baggage comes into view as soon as the topic of open marriages arises. Many people are totally okay with the sex but can't even begin to imagine the honesty part. Other people get hung up on the fact that I'm married, yet they feel perfectly comfortable cheating on their girlfriends or boyfriends. I've experienced a million different reactions of every variety and every combination of sticking points. But what all these people have in common is that they have an opinion about my marriage, regardless of whether it impacts them.

My choice to be honest with my partners outside my marriage is as important to me as being honest with Christopher. It's always fascinating to me that people are more disturbed by the idea of an open marriage than they are by cheating. Christopher and I talk a lot about what's behind other people's negative reactions to our relationship, and we work to separate out those reactions from our true feelings about our own marriage—feelings free of societal baggage and based on our instincts about, experience with, and understanding of sexuality and partnerships. Christopher is not a victim. He's a smart guy who knows that having sex with other people wouldn't be the thing to break us up. Sex is the easy part. And even if or when we develop feelings of love for someone else, consummating that relationship wouldn't be our demise, either. That is, sex is not the tipping point. We'd be no more likely to leave each other over having sex with someone else than over harboring feelings for another person whom we opted not to sleep with.

To play out this scenario a bit further, say we were simply interested in someone outside of our marriage. Say we longed for that person but chose not to act on that urge. The longing for that person would be likely to turn into a stronger desire if we didn't act on it, because we'd be feeding the mystery, the allure, of something we couldn't have. We can't stop each other from having the feelings we have, feelings that everyone has—married or not. Loving someone else is not going to change the love I have for my husband. This is hard for a lot of people to swallow. But why?

Sadly, I think it has to do with the fact that people are insecure in their relationships, which, in turn, is mostly because they are not self-confident. Low self-esteem pushes people to look to their partners to define them. If they then lose that partner, or if they can't confirm that they're their partner's one and only, then they lose their self-definition. But as long as they continue to live with the illusion that they are all their partner could ever want or need, they feel good about themselves. If your partner really is all you want and need, great. But I haven't found too many people for whom that's true. Regardless of the feelings my husband may have for other people, they don't change who I am or how we interact. I don't need Christopher to define me, and I definitely only love him more for being open to exploring this way of living with me—because it honors who I am and what I need, and he's not any worse off, either.

kyle and I went to a sushi restaurant

for dinner that night, and it was one of the best dates of my life. We were that couple whom everyone in the restaurant envies, laughing and flirting and generally reveling in each other's company. Because I didn't know him, I could simply enjoy him. Mitchell speaks to this experience when he writes, "What makes someone desirable is idealization, an act of imagination that highlights the qualities that make that person unique, special, out of the ordinary."[9] So yes, we desire those whom we don't and can't truly know. And yet at its core, the idealized version of a life partner is someone whom you get to know completely. How strange and unfortunate that we are primed to expect to get something from marriage that's so opposed to the laws of attraction and desire.

After dinner, we went back to my hotel room and talked and made out. It was amazingly comfortable. We knew the boundaries. It was new and different, and when I looked into Kyle's eyes, I saw a version of myself that made me feel sexy and amazing, which I didn't always feel when I was with Christopher. Not that it was his fault or mine or our marriage's—it just happens. I don't know that familiarity breeds contempt, but it certainly breeds familiarity. And that doesn't exactly lend itself to a woman's being seen as some sort of brilliant, gorgeous sex goddess. I'm human. I want to be seen. It's in my genes. I don't want to live without something I'm wired to want. Being with Kyle fed that part of me that gets the short end of the stick within a well-oiled marriage, the part of me that wants and likes to be idealized and adored, the part that likes sex for the sake of sex. I had no history with Kyle, and that felt good. Damn good, in fact.

He went off to a meeting the next morning, and we saw each other again later that day. I was going home that night, and he asked if he could see me again. It was hard for me to imagine that happening. We had different home cities, different schedules, our respective "real lives" waiting for us. Just the same, I was excited at the prospect of seeing him again. We kissed goodbye and I watched him drive away.

"How long have you two been together?" I turned around to face a woman who was standing nearby. She was in her twenties, pretty and bright eyed.

"I'm sorry. I just couldn't help but notice. You and your boyfriend look so cute together. You're so lucky. You can see from a mile away how much he adores you. I hope I find that one day." I didn't tell her the truth. I wanted to, but it would have been too much for a stranger to digest. I found it impossible not to listen to the part of me that whispered in my ear menacingly about how reckless it would be to espouse my ideas so willfully to impressionable minds. Besides, what would I say: *Are you kidding? That's not my boyfriend. That's my newest lover. We met two days ago. I'm married to a wonderful man. I live a gleefully uninhibited life that allows me the joys and security of a longtime commitment without barring me from experiencing the pleasures of new partners.*

Instead I said, "Thank you. It's been a year. He's sweet." It was a white lie to a woman I'd never see again, but one part of me felt my commitment to being honest coming unhinged. Luckily, I've squashed that voice since then, but back in the beginning, it always won out. Perhaps I still held out some hope that maybe I *was* a little crazy, that I just had to get something out of my system, and that monogamous marriage ultimately did hold all the keys to the kingdom. But now, I feel 100 percent sure that those ideas simply aren't true.

I only saw Kyle once again, although we talked on the phone once in a while and tried to meet up on several other occasions. We lived about five hours away from each other, and our schedules allowed only one other meeting before phone numbers were lost or lives changed or desires cooled. But the two times Kyle and I did sleep together, every second felt like a surprise. He told me again and again how much he loved my body, how beautiful I was. Do I think that? On good days, sure. Does my husband tell me that? Of course, sometimes. Is it still fantastic to hear, especially from a hot twenty-five-year-old? Uh, *yeah.* I have generally good self-esteem, and Christopher is relatively generous with compliments, but the context was completely different when Kyle said the very same words. It seems almost too simplistic, but there it is: We can become someone new again when we are with someone new. It's not a matter of wanting to do away with who we are; rather, it's about a desire to supplement who we are and what we have.

I can't help but wonder how much of this societal discussion about what types of sex and relationships are deemed "acceptable" (who the judge and jury are on that, I have no idea) has to do with simple distraction. It works splendidly as a means of keeping the real issues at bay. Examples of this avoidance are played out everywhere. Consider the fact that women are significantly more likely to suffer harm at the hands of a man they know, or are even in a relationship with, than a stranger's. Yet we are bombarded with images and messaging about fearing for our safety in the streets. What does it say about us as a society that we are obsessed with sensationalism? A lot of people think of open marriage as nothing more than some sort of freak show, a fringe lifestyle. However, people's lack of understanding, their often blatant unwillingness to comprehend it, is the very thing that keeps it so marginalized.

Keep people focused on "successful" marriages and stress the deviance, the downright vulgarity, of untraditional sexuality, and people have an insta-cause to get all up in arms about. Never mind rallying for better health insurance, demanding equality for the LGBTQ community, or fighting for better schools; expending countless resources and energy on bashing, dismissing, or pontificating about what people do behind closed doors is clearly a better way to spend our time. In her book *What Is Marriage For?* E. J. Graff argues, "What other arguments can you resort to when your ideology is outdated—except apocalyptic predictions of misery, disease, and God's wrath?"[10] The opponents of marriages like mine throw out theories like, "It will bring the end of marriage as we know it," because no rational argument against open marriage exists. Interesting how a means of saving or bettering, or even simply properly naming, a failing institution that, in many ways, is seen as the foundation of our society could be blamed for ultimately leading to the demise of the entire world as we know it.

You don't have to believe in some sort of far-out conspiracy theory to see that many people's current stand regarding family values and forbidding gays and lesbians to marry is very much about keeping powerful people in power. Graff concurs: "Marriage's boundaries are blurry. And exactly what counts as marriage changes according to whose interests are at stake."[11] In other words, as long as those authorities get to define my lifestyle choices as "slutty," and get to insist that I'm doomed, they're ensuring that other people worry more about avoiding these supposed "consequences" and protecting their "reputations," and less about their happiness or the state of our society at large. Distraction is a powerful weapon against that which we loathe or fear.

Christopher and I have determined, despite what others might say about the supposed selfishness, indulgence, or "having our cake and eating it, too" element of our situation, that it's not about them. It's not for others to worry about. Our sexual desire deserves our attention, and this is how we've chosen to manage it. For us, open marriage works. It would be nice if more people actually considered it a viable option, but we're not there yet. And so there are people like us, people like me, who've decided to live openly and speak honestly in an effort to both bust the myths and provide some visibility for a misunderstood and underrespected lifestyle. When I do tire of discussing my situation with yet another shocked and confused party, I try to remind myself of that. And when I react as I did to that woman who asked me if Kyle was my boyfriend—stifling the truth just because I didn't know her—I think, *Why would I?* I'm happy and unashamed. I am open with myself and others. My husband and I remain happily united—no betrayal, dishonesty, or false sense of self divides us. And so we continue on our journey of figuring it all out—not for the world, but for ourselves.

Chapter 7

you can't
run out of love

Soon she decided that she wanted to date only women outside her marriage. And it wasn't long before she met a young woman who became her friend, and then her lover. They fell in love and she wondered what that meant, or if it had to mean anything. Was she polyamorous? Was she a lesbian? Was she staying in her marriage for the wrong reasons—for comfort and convenience? In time, though, she realized that having an exclusive girlfriend was part of her larger journey.

having a series of out-of-town lovers
was fun for a while, but it wasn't without its problems. Despite every measure I took to practice safe sex, I still

worried about contracting something. And although I did my best to be sure I wasn't seeing anyone crazy or attached, my judgment of character failed me a time or two. And it wasn't as if a bevy of ideal suitors were lined up at my door. There were plenty of lulls, because I was quite selective about whom I dated. Christopher has never chosen to date anyone at all. His only dalliance was making out with a girl he met in a bar in L.A., which was out of character for him, as he's not one for public displays of affection.

In the beginning, I found myself needing to check in with him frequently, to ask whether he was still feeling okay about everything. He assured me, unequivocally, that he was, and that he rather enjoyed the side benefits of my trysts: I was happier and living more honestly, as well as off his back about many of the issues that had been troublesome for me before we opened our relationship. Many people who have never experienced an open relationship find it impossible to imagine that this type of arrangement can actually make the primary partners love each other more, but the truth is that it absolutely can, and for us, it absolutely does.

As time went on, I realized that I was much more interested in seeking out women than men. My sexual experiences with women were different from, and often better than, those I'd had with men. This certainly raised questions for me around my sexual identity, and plenty of people have asked me whether I opened my marriage simply because I wanted to be with women. It would be a lie if I said no, but I'm not convinced that I want to be with women because I'm a lesbian. Instead, I think it's because my sexuality, like that of many, many women, is more fluid than current definitions of "gay" and "straight" (or even "bisexual") allow.

Lisa M. Diamond is an associate professor of psychology and gender studies at the University of Utah. In her research, she explores distinctions between romantic love and sexual desire, as well as the nature of lesbian sexual identity as dynamic, rather than static. Her work, although focused primarily on women who identify as lesbian, suggests that women's sexual orientation is neither as unchanging nor as early-appearing a trait as some suggest. "Female same-sex orientations often exhibit late and abrupt development, and inconsistencies among women's prior and current behavior, ideation, and attractions have been extensively documented."[1]

In her book *Sexual Fluidity,* Diamond argues that current labels for sexual desire fall short, and including bisexuality as a qualifier to describe those who are somewhere in between doesn't solve the problem. She addresses questions about whether women even have a sexual orientation at all; whether a woman's sexuality is a choice; whether a woman who identifies as straight can fall in love with a woman, and if the reverse—if a woman who identifies as a lesbian can fall in love with a man—is possible as well; and whether women are sexually fluid throughout their lives. She suggests that for women, gender is not the issue—context is. As one's life and situation change, so too can one's sexuality and sexual identity evolve. Love relationships themselves, Diamond asserts, determine the gender women find themselves attracted to—at that point in time.[2]

So many things in life are about nuance and shifting and progression. Why, then, when it comes to sexuality and relationships, would they suddenly *not* be about gradation, but instead about goose-stepping into line with the rest of the flock? The cover story of *Newsweek*'s May 2007 issue, "The Mystery of Gender," was released because the media is finally paying attention to the fact that even gender is not necessarily a constant. We are finally coming to terms with the fact that "It's a boy!" or "It's a girl!" just might not cover it all. Biology clearly creates a symphony with innumerable combinations; it's not a solo act singing one thin tune.

I prefer to think of undefinable sexuality as being open to the idea that you might be able to have feelings for someone of the same gender, even if you've lived your whole life as a straight person. And that's what it's been like for me. I've always been amenable to listening to my sexuality. That's the point of all of this, really. It's not that open marriage is this one specific thing, with established rules and philosophies and ideas. Rather, it's a space that allows me and anyone else who inhabits it to be open—to people of both sexes; to having more than one committed partner at a time; to living in threes or fours or whatever works for the people involved; to being happy; and to changing all along the way.

My desire to be with women in the first place was a surprise to me. I was twenty-five when I had my first lesbian experience. Her name was Sophie Anne, and she was my best friend at the time. I suppose I'd had crushes on women before—a college professor and maybe a friend here or there. In college, particularly, the concept of a "political lesbian" resonated with me. Jennifer Baumgardner speaks to her own experiences in *Look Both Ways: Bisexual Politics:* "Women had sexual relationships with people they wanted to learn from and with whom they felt a spark. They did it because it felt right, and why should they miss out? They did it to make the best relationship they could, and to learn what a good relationship was."[3] Lots of women who get involved in relationships like these respond especially to their lack of preset roles. It can be freeing to be with another woman because gender roles, which can be incredibly oppressive for women, simply disappear. Suddenly everything has to be—or gets to be—negotiated from ground zero.

And despite the fact that some lesbian relationships appear to have masculine and feminine roles (that is, butch/femme distinctions), those roles can still be freely defined in ways that are meaningful to that particular couple. One may have short hair and one may have long hair. One may drive a truck and the other a sedan. But who takes out the trash and who cooks dinner is not automatically assigned, the way it is within heterosexual couples. Everything has to be negotiated. "Butch-femme is not about aping traditional notions of masculinity and femininity any more than it is about mimicking heterosexuality," explains Jeannine DeLombard in her essay "Femmenism."[4] It's a whole new ball game, and I like playing it.

"Who's the boy?" Jemma sometimes asked me, early on in our relationship. "Do I have to be, since I'm taller and stronger than you?" The answer we discovered was, and is, of course not. We both do the things we want to and are capable of, not simply the things that gender stereotypes dictate to us. She carries the suitcases and I cook dinner. She picks out our outfits and I fix the clogged sink. And making those choices feels like we are actually making choices. It's not a matter of somehow doing something wrong or failing to fill preordained roles. It isn't connected to inadequacy at all; it's connected to workability. But it is something we have to consciously figure out for ourselves, not something that's laid out for us. DeLombard explains, "Butch-femme is nothing if not intricate, subtle, and highly complex, despite the fact that it is often oversimplified as a monolithic set of prescribed, restrictive behaviors by straight people and lesbians alike."[5] It's not as easy as who's the boy and who's the girl, but it is amazingly rewarding.

We do what works, and that is what I have learned in and love about the relationships I have had with women. Partnerships work best when people are true to themselves, and that is the only thing to be true to when the couple is made up of two people of the same sex. Is this always true? Of course not. But it certainly is what I have witnessed and experienced.

And what I have learned from my open marriage is that restrictions regarding perceived male and female identities don't *have* to play a part in heterosexual relationships, either. Though some people see open relationships as a corruption or loss of "traditional" values, mine has allowed me to question, loosen, and realign the invalid gender guidelines that bind so many straight women to dysfunctional relationships.

I have always felt aligned with the lesbian community's politics and worldview. In college, that might have been because most of the feminists I knew were also lesbians. I identified as a feminist at that point in my life, given my own liberal views on sex as I started college. And the fact that I didn't pursue sexual relationships with women back then strikes me as curious. It just didn't occur to me, but I understand now that it couldn't have, because every societal indicator was pointing me toward being with men. Why else wouldn't I have explored the idea sooner? I was plenty experimental in the sexual realm, and pornography that featured women together turned me on. Still, it didn't fall into my lap until I met Sophie Anne.

For me, being with a woman was a true awakening, in that it gave me new insight into how a relationship could be. "Women who looked both ways learned from women how to get what we wanted from a relationship—information that we could, if inclined, use to have more satisfying and equal relationships with men," writes Baumgardner.[6] And sexually, it was an entirely new ball of wax. There is something so particular about being with another woman—how soft her skin is, how curvy her body is, how circular the sex is. And there's no race to the "finish line" with women. No matter how sensitive or capable a man might be, when he comes, the party is pretty much over. Not so with another woman.

Having sex with a woman didn't make me want to rush to identify as one thing or another. But I was clearly attracted to women, and I was fine with the fact that that meant I was bisexual. Still, I don't care much for that word, and I know I'm not alone, as Diamond's research shows. The term "bisexual" doesn't feel right to a lot of women, perhaps because being bisexual has become almost passé, or perhaps, as Baumgardner explains, because "as a label, 'bisexual' sounds pathological, academic, and a little embarrassed—like the identities 'stay-at-home mom' and 'runner-up.'"[7] This is precisely how I feel when I hear myself say the word—like it's not quite right, or *I'm* not quite right, or I'm two things when I should be one. Bisexuality has gotten a bad rap over the years because it carries a stigma that those of us who are attracted to both sexes somehow want more than our share, or more than what's normal.

Today, being gay is more acceptable—at least in most parts of the country—than it's ever been, but for some, bisexuality still connotes people who don't have their shit figured out. But I beg to differ. "The living world is a continuum in each and every one of its aspects," wrote Kinsey in 1948, articulating his theory of sexual fluidity.[8] If that continuum were a scale from one to ten, with one representing heterosexuality and ten representing homosexuality, I'd probably put myself at seven. And most people, whether they can admit it or not, do not fall on the one or the ten. The majority of us fall somewhere in between because we're all bisexual to some degree. I'm not suggesting that everyone therefore wants to or should change their sexual behavior; it simply means that our rigidity surrounding labels and our desire to ascertain some sort of fixed sexual identity for ourselves and others is a great big waste of time and energy, especially if Diamond is correct—and I believe she is—that women's sexuality is always subject to change.

Even though I have started identifying as bisexual, for lack of a better word, it would be nice if that weren't necessary, but the world we live in is very label oriented, and people desperately want everyone neatly categorized, perhaps because it makes them feel safer. Regardless, whether I named it or not, my attraction to women played a role in my inability to feel satisfied in my marriage as it was. I continue to wonder sometimes whether I am a lesbian. But if I were, would that negate this discussion of openness and polyamory? Would my quandary simply disappear if I were attracted to only one gender or the other? I don't know. All

I know is that at first, being with one man—my husband—
made me think I still wanted to be with other men. But, after
trying that out, being with other men only made me long for
other women. I got to a point where I thought perhaps the
"more" I was looking for was just being with women, and I
knew of only one way to find out.

meeting women, in a very practical

sense, proved to be much harder than meeting men. I simply
didn't know how or where to pick up a woman. Hanging
out, as I did, in places that weren't necessarily gay or straight
meant trying to figure out which women might be interested.
And since I am generally attracted to femme women, fewer
indicators—as stereotypical as those indicators might be—
existed to help me determine potential partners.

When I did seek out lesbian venues, I faced the possibility
that my bisexuality would be problematic for the women I
ended up talking to. Not to mention that I was also married.
Throw that into the mix, and I was going to have to find some
pretty open-minded women. Ultimately, I was looking for
attractive, smart, witty women who would also understand
and be okay with my situation. Not an easy task. But don't
assume that the central issue was the fact that women aren't
interested in sex outside of the promise of a commitment.
That isn't the case at all.

I figured I couldn't possibly be the first person in this type
of situation. So, as I often do when I am feeling perplexed

about something in life, I decided to see if there might be any books to help me figure it out. Lo and behold, I found a book whose title suggested that I might have found exactly what I was looking for: *The Straight Girl's Guide to Sleeping with Chicks,* by Jen Sincero. Although I'd been with women before and was as opposed to being labeled "straight" as I was to being deemed "bi," I was pretty sure the references would apply. The very fact that the book existed spoke to the fact that I wasn't alone on the planet. There were other "straight girls" who wanted to figure out how to meet other "chicks"—and, yes, sleep with them. It helped, too, that Sincero approached the subject with a heavy dose of humor and chutzpah.

Knowing that these women were out there, coupled with my new resolve to find them, resulted in one false start—a very nice girl who came back to my hotel room and then became uneasy when she realized what she'd gotten into—and several very fun nights that busted the myth that women aren't interested in sex for the sake of sex—with other women. One of those women was someone I met at yet another writers' conference in 2004. I started up a conversation with my waiter, Thomas, who asked me if I wanted to go out for a drink with him when he got off his shift. I had no idea what his intentions were, but he was funny and friendly, and it seemed like we could have a good time together, even though I wasn't seeking his affections. And so I asked him, "Actually, do you know anything about the gay and lesbian scene around here?"

"Oh," he said.

"Yeah," I smiled.

"Well, you're in luck, because it just so happens that I do." Turned out Thomas was a struggling actor and had a ton of gay friends. "I know just the place," he said. After making him promise me that he had no illusions of a threesome (only partially in jest), I jumped into a cab with him. The taxi stopped in front of a small, dark club. Plush and hip. Thomas introduced me to his friends, and then walked right up to the bartender and told him what I was looking for. I was mortified—until the bartender introduced me to Justine. She was lean and about five inches taller than I was, with attentive eyes and a great smile. Her long arms were covered in tattoos of angels, and her blond hair was cut in a perfect pixie. I was smitten.

We talked and flirted, and after a few hours, the talking turned to kissing and I began wondering if I would ever have the nerve to ask her to go back to my room with me. I can be the tiniest bit impulsive, especially when I get nervous and have had a few martinis. So I somehow found myself blurting, "Is now when I ask if you want to come back to my hotel?" She smiled and giggled.

"I thought you'd never ask," she said. I laughed in relief and asked the bartender to call us a cab.

On the way back to my room, we had a chance to talk more, and Justine told me that she hadn't been with a woman in a long time. I was completely surprised to find out that she had three kids and had been dating men exclusively for quite some time. Because of where we'd met, the fact that the bartender had "referred" her to me, and her look, I'd automatically assumed she was gay. Shame on me. The social brainwashing rages on.

We had fun that night. Justine was so alternative looking compared to me, and I loved it. Her nipples were pierced, and parts of her body that had been covered by clothes in the bar turned out to be covered in more tattoos. We laughed and talked and kissed and played, and then, at 5:00 a.m., she headed out to relieve her babysitter and be sure she was home before her girls woke up. We made plans to talk again, which we did once after I got back home. But it was definitely just one of those things. Christopher ate up the story when I told him about it; he asked for more and more details, which was generally how it went. When I was with a man, he wanted to know that it had happened, but nothing more; when I was with a woman, he wanted the whole megillah—and it always turned him on.

With Christopher's interest fueling my own, our relationship felt more lively and exciting than ever, perhaps even more so than it had when we were first dating. I dated another married woman in the winter of 2005, who told me that her experiences with me had the same effect on her and her husband. "I couldn't wait for my husband to come home," she told me after we had been together. "I felt so sexy. I just wanted to attack him." Another married couple I was with both told me some time afterward that their encounter with me had revved up their sex life and their desire for each other. These scenarios seem to remind couples that their partners are desirable to other people. It intrigues me that so many people fear that the exact opposite will transpire. Not so, in my experience.

eventually, even dating only women,

I started to believe that maintaining a series of multiple partners wasn't what I envisioned for myself ultimately. That was when the second leg of my journey began, when I started to explore not just the sexual-freedom side of open marriage, but the polyamorous side as well. I got a girlfriend.

I met Jemma when I was working on a review of an art show opening at a local gallery. She was the gallery's curator, and she gave me a tour of the exhibit. She invited me to a lecture by the artist that night, and afterward we went out for drinks with some of her friends. I liked her. She was smart and funny, pretty and stylish. Not my usual type. Too young. And too sweet. I had a penchant for women with tattoos, women whose personas were anything but sweet. Jemma was twenty-six, and as innocent and straitlaced as they come. Think cheerleader and class valedictorian. Think Reese Witherspoon, not Salma Hayek.

But we had such a great time together, and we had so much in common. Jemma started inviting me out more regularly, sometimes with her friends in tow, sometimes alone. We were friends at first, and I didn't even consider that we might be more than that. The fact that she lived in town meant that dating her would break one of the rules Christopher and I had set. And she was straight. "Very straight," she told me one night, after I asked her if she'd ever consider dating women.

Not too far into our friendship, I decided it was time for me to explain my situation to Jemma and a few of her friends whom I'd been out with a couple of times before. We were headed to a bar, and I didn't want her to get the wrong idea if she saw me flirting with anyone. I figured she would likely misconstrue it as either cheating or pursuing cheating.

"Look, I hope this isn't TMI," I said over dinner, "but Christopher and I are allowed to sleep with other people. We're in an open marriage. And I'm also bi."

They seemed surprised but not shocked. They were fine with it—for me—but they all concurred that it wasn't for them.

"Well, wait till you're married for a while," I told the group of twentysomethings seated around me. "And wait until you meet a woman who makes you forget that you don't like women. Then decide how monogamous and straight you are." They just laughed. But I wasn't joking. There I was, at a table filled with attractive, self-confident, accomplished women, most of them more than ten years younger than I, all of them subscribing to the same beliefs I'd had at their age. It was amazing. I had to think about that same point in my own life, when I felt as if everything would unfold in a certain way. I wondered if perhaps the fact that my life had turned out so differently from the Disneyfied version I'd anticipated helped me relate better to these girls. Or maybe no amount of explaining could allow them to identify with what was more likely to be their own experience down the road than they would have liked to admit. It's a funny place to be in—almost like being able to see the future.

I felt compelled to share my situation with them because I never want anyone to think, *Poor Christopher,* or to think badly of me. I understand that they might think badly of me regardless, but at least I'd be living as honestly and openly as I know how to. And I'd rather have someone disagree with my choices than make assumptions about me without even being aware of those choices.

Jemma and her friends asked a few questions about how it all started, how it worked, and how I realized I was bi. No judgment, just curiosity. By and large, this has been my experience when I confide in younger women. I think that (in general, anyway) each generation is more open-minded than the next. Young woman today seem particularly interested in discovering the world for themselves, rather than having it force-fed to them. They are looking for new recipes for finding happiness, and they are not afraid to think for themselves and to experiment, accepting their own experiences and their peers' experiences as truth. They seem far less willing to embrace "That's just the way it is" as an explanation for the way the world works. They want to *see* it work.

It wasn't long before Jemma and I were spending a lot of time together. We had a lot in common, and she was willing to be my "plus-one" for the many events I had to attend that Christopher would sooner have pulled all his teeth out than sign on for. We also became each other's confidant. There wasn't anything we didn't talk about, and she was one of the few people I shared "Portrait of an Open Marriage" with, the piece I wrote about my marriage for *Tango* magazine. That article sparked a lot of conversations between us about sexuality and couples and romance. The more she told me, the closer I felt to her—and she to me.

Although Jemma's story wasn't my own, it was familiar—maybe simply because we are both women and have therefore both struggled with the same issues, no matter how different our experiences might have been. She didn't lose her virginity until she was twenty-two, has had very few sexual partners, and had never even considered being with a woman, let alone actually gone through with it. But many women I know, regardless of their specific sexual and romantic backgrounds, are so baffled by mixed messages, signals, and expectations that they find themselves in relationships and marriages that leave them confused and dissatisfied. All of that conflicting information I spoke about earlier in this book makes it very difficult for young women to sort out who they are and what they want, especially when it comes to matters of the heart and desires of the body. As different as Jemma and I are, we are very similar in certain ways. We both wanted (and want) what I think all women do: happy, healthy, satisfying, fulfilling, supportive, loving relationships with great sex.

"What about love?" she asked one day when we were discussing how my open marriage in particular worked. I told her the truth.

"I don't know," I told her. "I don't know what would happen if I had other love relationships outside of my marriage." Up until that point, I had considered only the possibility of falling in love, and somehow I didn't expect it to actually happen. But it did, of course—I fell in love with Jemma. We went out of town one weekend a few months after we met, and she confessed, shyly, that she was interested in me. She asked me to kiss her and I did.

Jemma and I have been together for a year and a half as of this writing. I understand that she is that "something else" I was looking for to supplement my marriage. She's now the only person I see outside of my marriage. She is the only one I want to see, and she says she wouldn't be comfortable—not at this point in our relationship, anyway—with my seeing anyone else. She's not interested in dating anyone else, either. It seems altogether strange and amazingly simple.

And it works. Could I be happy with Jemma exclusively? I suppose that's possible. But I have no interest in leaving my husband. I think I will probably always desire more than what one person can possibly be for any other person.

I think it's likely that if Jemma and I attempted exclusivity, things would change for us; there would be a shift once we had the sense that I "had" her, once we had a mortgage to share and dishes to wash. I think the nature of our relationship would alter significantly. And I—we— don't want that. As it is now, it's relatively uncomplicated. I'm not sure I want to be in some sort of communal living situation, or if I could handle a stable full of people and all the permutations in which those people got together. But my having a husband and a girlfriend works for all of us. Right now, each of us has what we want and need. Will that change? I'm sure. But that's the benefit of being open: We follow love, desire, instinct, and honesty, rather than convention. And we remain open to exploring how the future unfolds.

before I fell in love with Jemma, I

had long argued that being open worked because it was strictly about sex. But then I found love. I still sometimes struggle to explain it to myself, let alone to other people. If open marriage works because it involves "just sex," then how can I reconcile my relationship with Jemma? How do I justify giving up sleeping with anyone else besides her outside of my marriage? How do I rationalize loving her, being in love with her? After questioning and requestioning myself, I've realized that falling in love with Jemma didn't contradict everything I'd always professed was true of open marriage. The thing I have with Jemma would be there whether or not we were sleeping together. Our emotional connection runs far deeper than the physical. The sex, albeit great, is still just sex. The feelings I have for her would be the same without it, and they wouldn't be any different if I chose not to acknowledge them to Christopher. In which case, it might look like a crush to Christopher. In fact, that might be exactly what it looks like to others who don't know about our situation. Regardless of what people know, Jemma's and my relationship may appear different to them, perhaps as something deeper or stronger than an average friendship. In most cases, women don't hang out with their female friends and call it cheating. But isn't it, in a way? Couldn't it be if you looked at it differently, if you considered the fact that you'd rather hang out with your girlfriend than your husband? Or that your girlfriend is your travel companion, your plus-one, your confidant in matters of the heart?

I think many women, whether they are willing to admit to it or not, have greater intimacy with their best friends than they do with their husbands. It's culturally accepted, and that makes it okay. And thank God for that! But wouldn't it seem more logical for men to be more threatened by their wives' best friends than by men who hit on their wives?

Those guys don't pose nearly the same threat of providing the kind of closeness that so many women crave, and that they are likely getting already from their female friends. The reason men aren't threatened, generally, is that they don't fear not being the person who's closest to their wife's mind. Instead, they fear losing ownership of her body, which doesn't belong to them in the first place.

Sex doesn't make the intimacy. The intimacy is there, and sex enhances it. Intimacy is expressed differently in various relationships. I adored Jemma before I slept with her, and I adore her still. We have both said, many times, that the happiest thing for both of us is that we feel confident that we will still love each other and be there for each other if and when sex stops being part of our equation. Open marriage, for me, is about having enough love to go around; it's about finding all of the love and closeness and sex I desire in a way that doesn't hurt anyone involved.

I know that for me, being with Christopher and resenting every minute of it because I'd rather be somewhere else, with someone else, would be far more hurtful—to both of us. Being with your spouse while you're telling someone else that you wish you could be with them can tear a relationship apart. The sex is not the problem; the unresolved feelings are. I'll be honest: I don't believe in soul mates, or that there is one person out there who's meant for each of us. Instead, I believe that we are capable of loving and being loved as much as we allow ourselves to.

Sex is just sex. Can you feel closer to someone by having it? Certainly. But not necessarily. Strangely, sexual love is often elevated over platonic love, and yet the opposite should be true. It's easy to be "in love" with someone you're having sex with. Sex is the best drug, bar none. But feeling love across a Scrabble board, feeling a connection for no specific reason at no specific time—isn't that the love that should seem more unusual? More valued? Look, if it's up to me, I say give all love the same value and stop trying to privilege any one love over another. And allow sex to be what it is: a joyous physical activity that can express levels of intimacy from zero to sixty.

Once again, language is a major barrier here. The Greeks had a number of words for love. *Eros. Philos. Agape. Storge.* We have one. One lousy word to describe a plethora of feelings and relationships. That fact goes hand in hand with Americans' limited thinking that the only relationship that really "counts" is monogamous, heterosexual marriage. The irony is that there is no *one* love, and there is no *one* kind of relationship.

My partnership with Jemma no longer feels surprising; it's no longer a contradiction in my journey. It is another spot on the spectrum of relationships that coincides harmoniously with my marriage. We need different things at different times. The problem with modern marriage is that it simply does not allow for the fact that relationships aren't static. People aren't static. Sexuality isn't static. So why should marriage be?

Chapter 8

it's not necessarily what you think

It became increasingly clear that open marriage is not what most people think. People thought she was promiscuous, or that she hosted orgies, or that her daughter saw her with other people. Some people thought she and her husband were immoral, and that the only way to live was in a monogamous, heterosexual marriage. Some people thought she was selfish and a bad mother. But she and her husband knew that their marriage looked like most people's marriages—except that they were honest with each other, and they were happier than they'd ever been.

too many people have preconceived notions about open marriage. Open marriage is, by definition, open, which means it can and does take any number of forms: It can be a triad of two women and one man, or vice versa. It can be a quad of any mix. It can include couples with children and without, people who live alone, and people for whom sex is the only thing they share with someone other than their spouse. For others, it's about love. But most important, it's not limited to a certain type of picture or a certain type of couple. We are not all porn stars or career sex writers. We are not people whom you'd automatically peg as being interested in wildly alternative scenarios. Rather, open marriages often look startlingly similar to the majority of traditional marriages you encounter every day—one man and one woman with one or two kids, living in the suburbs with no strange cars parked out front and no drama spilling out back.

Open marriage doesn't imply anything beyond the fact that my husband and I have partners outside of each other, one of whom we shared (and that was the only time). It's embarrassingly simple, really. People think it's a lot more exciting, edgy, or controversial than it is. Plenty of more unusual, complicated, and taboo things are brewing in other people's bedrooms. Married, single, divorced—it doesn't preclude people from doing kinky things. And open marriages may or may not be kinky. They're more reflective of each person's, and thereby each couple's, identity. Ours is generally incredibly tame, although at other times, I've acted on fantasies that have been extremely exciting.

Our situation has worked like this: I go out of town and I'm open to the possibility of a sexual encounter. Christopher is allowed the same freedom, although he says he's too shy to partake. Knowing him as I do, I would guess it's more about his not "needing" such an opportunity. But he's told me that if I brought someone home and we had a mutual interest in her, he wouldn't turn her away. This prospect applies only to women, as Christopher has expressed time and again that he is not interested in being in a threesome with another man. Christopher talks openly about homosexuality. He knows I'm interested in women, after all, and that I identify as bisexual. Yet the idea of my bringing another man home is not an option in our relationship. And that's perfectly fine with me.

I came across a tidbit in the book *The Sexual Spectrum,* by Dr. Olive Johnson, that made me laugh when I read it, in part because it made me think about just how uncomfortable with homosexuality many men truly are. In 1996, psychologist Henry Adams and some of his colleagues from the University of Georgia investigated erotic arousal in a group of straight men who admitted that they had negative feelings toward homosexuals. The researchers compared these homophobic men to nonhomophobic ones—that is, men who said they had no negative feelings toward homosexuals. Both groups were shown sexually explicit videos of heterosexuals, lesbians, and gay men, while their penile arousal was measured by a plethysmograph. The results? Both groups of men were sexually aroused by videos of both straight and lesbian women, but *only* the homophobic men became aroused by male homosexual videos.[1]

For Christopher, it seems that the freedom to be with other people interests him more than actually acting on it. It's that "I could if I wanted to" mentality. As it turns out right now, because of my steady relationship with Jemma, Christopher and I are also in a very steady and stable, albeit open, marriage. I see Jemma when I can, and Christopher remains "single," as it were, outside of our relationship. I choose not to be open to a sexual encounter beyond Jemma and Christopher because that is what both Jemma and I want. The complexity of being in an open relationship is that you have to continually negotiate the terms with each partner. Christopher and I had already established that I could date whomever I wanted within the boundaries of our agreement, and he was happy to lift the out-of-town-only rule because he knew and liked and felt comfortable with Jemma. She and I, however, have chosen together to be mutually exclusive (other than my being with Christopher, of course), and so that, for the moment, is the primary ground rule of our relationship.

Jemma often hangs out at our house, and I presume the neighbors think she's my best friend (if they think anything of it at all). And they wouldn't be wrong. I just happen to sleep with her as well. I love and trust Jemma. And what makes our dynamic even stronger is the fact that if we were to break up, the only thing that would be lost would be the sexual component of our relationship. Sadly, I think the same could have been true of my relationship with Grace, except for the fact that her husband didn't "allow" us to maintain a friendship, and she obliged.

The very best thing about open marriage is that it's exactly the opposite of what most people think it is. It is not subversive. It is not alternative. It is not countercultural or deviant. So go ahead and breathe. If you were worried that the only way you could be open to open marriage would be by putting a sex swing in your living room and going to swingers' retreats, fear not. Maybe you simply find yourself wanting something more or something other than your spouse when it comes to sex. Maybe you have come to accept that our hearts expand when we have more people to love. Maybe you're ready to let biology and reality, as opposed to religious dogma and social expectations, guide your way of life. It's okay—because open marriage looks however you want it to look.

one common misconception about open marriage is that it automatically implies loose morals. But it's quite the opposite, actually: It involves a heightened sense of ethics because it's all about honesty and openness. Sex and morality, much like sex and marriage, have gotten dangerously jumbled. Just for the fun of it, let's take a look at what "morality" means *The Stanford University Encyclopedia of Philosophy* defines it like this:

The term "morality" can be used either:

1. descriptively to refer to a code of conduct put forward by a society or,

a. some other group, such as a religion, or

b. accepted by an individual for her own behavior or

2. normatively to refer to a code of conduct that, given specified conditions, would be put forward by all rational persons.[2]

Let's begin with the first definition. What society, group, religion, or individual gets to set the moral standard? And if we have no common morality, which we surely don't, then why should open marriage imply a lack thereof? If you're thinking this is merely an argument of the slippery-slope variety, then you might look at it this way instead: If open marriage suggests compromised morals, then what about sex toys, anal sex, S&M, fetishes, and so on? Where is the line? Who decides? It seems to me that open marriage gets short shrift because people don't know anything about it, so it's an easy target for them to project their assumptions on to.

Dossie Easton and Catherine A. Liszt take on this issue in *The Ethical Slut*. They begin their exploration by "taking back" the word "slut." They suggest using it not as a means of judgment, but instead as an indication of freedom and ownership of one's own sexuality. They write, "We are proud to reclaim the word 'slut' as a term of approval, even endearment."[3] Hereby, the two suggest that we, as a society, determine what our morals and ethics should be and how they ought to drive us. Our morals are not absolutes. They have everything to do with perceptions, and the words and definitions we choose for ourselves.

Albert Einstein once said, "A man's ethical behavior should be based effectually on sympathy, education, and social ties; no religious basis is necessary. Man would indeed be in a poor way if he had to be restrained by fear of punishment and hope of reward after death."[4] So many people act based only on their fear of retribution, and yet here's Einstein, someone whose genius I think nearly everyone could agree on, making the brilliant point that we don't need religion enforcing behavioral guidelines for us; we do, however, need to learn to be more civil. If we acted more as Einstein suggests we do, we would be open to the fact that there are many ways to experience life and love. We would embrace lifestyles and relationships that fall outside of the traditional and the standard. We would evolve.

Another travesty that is too often ignored when it comes to this morality debate is how women inevitably end up on the losing side. "If you ask about a man's morals," write Easton and Liszt, "you will probably hear about his honesty, loyalty, integrity, and high principles. If you ask about a woman's morals, you are more likely to hear about who she fucks and under what conditions."[5] This double standard is yet another weapon of misogyny's great warriors. Want to keep women obedient to men? Tell them that they're worthless if they listen to their own moral compass when it comes to their sexuality. It's certainly worked so far.

Open marriage isn't about loose morals. I'm not sure it's about morals at all. Morality is a social construct, while the principles behind open marriage are biologically based. We are not all wired for one lifestyle, which is why I'm suggesting that open marriage should be no less of an option than serial monogamy, homosexuality, lifetime abstinence, staying single, or having kids on one's own. Excuse me for calling in the big guns, but isn't this what our founding fathers had in mind in the first place—freedom of choice? If you can pick your religion, why would it make any less sense to choose your lifestyle in terms of whom you live with, love with, and sleep with?

because I have a daughter, it's impor-
tant to me to address the issue of parenting, and motherhood more specifically. Whenever the subject of my open marriage comes up, people always ask me, "But what about your daughter?" The implication seems to be that being in an open marriage automatically equals bad parenting. But my daughter knows nothing about my sex life. What my husband and I choose to do with our sex lives outside of

our commitment to each other is not something we're sharing with Emily, who, at the time of this writing, is eight
years old. The only people who have ever slept over at
our house are Lisbeth and Jemma, and they slept over before any sexual relationship developed. They were friends
first. We have never had strangers sleep over at our house.
We have never had orgies or wild parties, in part because
we're not interested in that, but more important because
we would not subject our daughter to behavior that would
be inappropriate because of her age, and because we're her
parents. Most couples who are in open relationships and
have children exist along the same spectrum of couples
who are not in open relationships and have children. Some
parents put their children first; others make poor choices
and selfish decisions.

Christopher and I established early on how we would
approach this issue with our daughter, and we decided that
we would just be ourselves, and would continue to parent as
we always had—by putting Emily first. In a wonderful essay
for Babble.com, writer Miriam Axel Lute, who is a mother
and is also in an open marriage, speaks to this point. "Still,
in my world and in the worlds of the other polyamorous
parents I know, all these challenges generally just mean
more time is focused on family and parenting. So it always
brings me up a little short to see people trotting out the
'clearly bad for children' argument about my family."[6] And
there you have it. Because we have what is considered an

"alternative" scenario, we think *more* about how everything—everything—affects our daughter.

What's normal to kids is whatever's presented as normal. We want Emily to think it's perfectly normal for friends to stay over. We want her to think it's perfectly normal that lots of people love her and love us—in a purely platonic way, of course—and for people to hug and cuddle and be together. And so she does, because that is what she sees.

And that is all she sees. She's never seen me kiss Jemma in a romantic way. When I stay at Jemma's house, I tell Emily the truth she needs to hear—that Jemma lives downtown and it's a matter of convenience. It's easier for me, and I don't miss out on being with my daughter any more than I would otherwise, since she would be asleep if I were to come home late. Lute explains, "The kids I know whose parents just have open marriages don't even really register it, and why should they? There's no reason it has to be any different to them if Mom gets an evening out to see her lover or to play cribbage."[7] And it isn't. I am away from Christopher more often than I might be, perhaps, but being in an open marriage does create some needed distance—space and time away included. And I can assure you he doesn't mind having the bed all to himself from time to time.

I stay with Jemma because I want to be with her and spend the night with her. I tell Emily that I spend time with Jemma because she is my best friend, and that it's just like Emily's wanting to be with her best friend. Would you call that lying by way of omission? Perhaps. But lying through omission is just one of the many components of good parenting. Your kids don't need to know if you had way too much to drink at that party last night, kissed someone you were interested in at work, or even had sex last night with your spouse.

For those who argue (and many people have) that I'm keeping Emily in the dark out of some sense of shame, I would ask this: Should children be exposed to their parents' porn library or sex-toy collection or dungeon? Of course not. And why shouldn't they be? It's not because those parents think what they are doing is wrong—nor should they. It's because children have no business knowing about or seeing that stuff. My daughter doesn't know anything about sex at this point, except that it's something grownups do. She is exposed to nothing more than any child of parents in a traditional marriage is, and arguably less than the children of parents who are single and dating.

Guess what else our daughter doesn't see? Fighting and resentment and unhappy parents, which children should be protected from. What kids shouldn't be hidden away from is love, and that's all our daughter witnesses—from us and from friends and family members who come to our home. And aren't love and support what everyone agrees children need more of? Lute explains it like this: "Yes, lovers/step-parents constantly coming and going and families falling apart and reforming at the drop of a hat certainly sounds like a less than ideal environment for children to me. But this is just what monogamous people imagine polyamory must be, just like straight people for so long imagined that gay people did nothing but have sex."[8] As Lute suggests, the very people making negative comments about poly families are quite often the ones having the experiences that truly harm impressionable young people. Lashing out at families that look different is as wrong, hurtful, and unfounded as it is easy.

If I needed any proof that our daughter has no idea that her parents' marriage is different from any other marriage she's privy to, I got it recently after watching the film *Arctic Tale* with her. The movie tells the story of two polar bear cubs and one walrus calf growing up in the wild. It's about global warming. But it's also about animal life cycles—and it therefore got my little one's mind a-turnin' about love, flirting, relationships, and where babies come from. At one point in the film, the "teenage" animals become sexually interested in other animals and begin their courting rituals.

"Why do people date when they're teenagers?" Emily asked me.

"Well, I guess because that's usually when people start thinking that they might like to have a boyfriend or a girlfriend," I told her.

"Well, Jemma is twenty-six and she doesn't have a boyfriend. Does that mean she can just keep dating?"

"If she wants to," I said, barely able to hold back a smile. "And she can date as much and for as long as she likes."

"Oh," Emily said, satisfied with my response and re-engrossed in the film.

And with that brief exchange, I saw that she sees Jemma and me as best friends and nothing more. Jemma is a great influence on Emily, too, and so Christopher and I can rest assured that whatever we are all doing is not only working for us, but also succeeding without affecting Emily. Morality and values for me are about trusting my gut to tell me what is contextually, fairly, and honestly "right," instead of blindly following universal and deceptive rules that are wrong. It's about evaluating situations and consequences more—realizing how the world really operates—and thinking less about what a church or someone touting the family-values agenda of the Republican Party says to do lest we burn in hell.

Can it really be moral to beat or kill someone because of whom they love? Can it ever be ethical to deny rights to people because of the living arrangements they choose? Is hate really a family value? I don't think so. And I don't want to live in a world that thinks so. That lack of critical thinking seems to be our biggest problem when it comes to this morality question. I'm not in an open marriage because someone told me that's the "right" thing to do, but because it's where thinking and experience have brought me. And that is my definition of values and ethics: looking at the bigger picture and examining, truthfully, how I fit into it.

Unfortunately, I can make all the philosophical arguments I want, and there will still be people who don't even know me waiting in line to call me a bad mother. And as if that isn't enough in the realm of morality, I've also mentioned the other accusations that have been liberally thrown at me: of being consumed by sex, of being an addict, even. What's particularly ironic is that I was actually much more focused on sex *before* I began exploring the idea of open marriage than I am now. Why? Because I wasn't satisfied. Now that I am, I have more time and energy and brainpower to put to use in other ways—from parenting to traveling to writing. This situation is not dissimilar to the nose job I got in college. Before that surgery, all I thought about was my nose—how big it was, how people must always be looking at it, how hideous I thought it made me look. But once I had the surgery, I didn't give it a second thought. I feel exactly the same way about my sex life. Before I considered this whole open-relationship thing, when I was on the verge of losing it and thinking about leaving Christopher and uprooting my whole life, thinking about sex consumed me. Now I am entirely at ease. I am happy and content with my life and the direction it's taking. Go figure.

We obsess over those things we long for. Fulfill that longing and *poof*—our obsession is gone. This concept is applicable to healthy obsessions only, and I use the word "obsession" in a purely nonclinical sense. If you're wondering what makes a healthy obsession, a good test is to ask yourself

whether, once quelled, it is feeding you or merely growing
into a deeper infatuation. Consider the following obsessions,
any of which might be healthy or unhealthy: plastic surgery,
tattoos, eating, or sex. If you get your Brazilian butt lift or
your tattoo, or if you eat that thing you've been craving or
have sex with whomever you've been wanting to have sex
with, and you feel good, content, full, finished, then that's
probably a healthy thing that you were simply really into,
perhaps a little possessed by, but not to the point of your
needing clinical help. But if you do any of these things and
they simply leave you feeling out of control, unable to stop,
and wanting more, more, more, then you might need to
consider what's really going on. I know that I don't want
more and more and more. Where sex is concerned, I just
want more than my husband. For a while, that meant a few
men a year. For now, that means one other woman. I have
absolutely no desire for anyone else. And I have no reason
not to be completely honest about that—which I know is a
huge luxury.

Trying to keep your obsessions in check is a lot like
dieting. That's why all those crazy fad diets don't work,
and why a program like Weight Watchers does. You cannot
completely and irrevocably deny yourself something,
especially something that you love, and expect to walk
away unscathed. It will catch up to you. Instead, indulge
in moderation. Lead your life in a reasonable fashion that
doesn't work against your biology, and (no surprise here)

that thing will no longer rule your life. Think of open marriage as Weight Watchers: Nothing is off-limits. You just have to work out a plan that works for you—or, in the case of open marriage, you and your partners.

I write better, sleep better, parent better, eat better— you get the idea—because I am not always wondering what else I could have, what I might be missing out on. I'm not constantly wondering whether I should leave my husband because I'm not fulfilled. I can have whatever "else" I want, and just knowing that makes me not dwell on it. Open marriage is not about leading a life focused on sex; it's about leading a life free from fretting about it. And for me, it's been about liberating myself from focusing inward to a degree that was destructive to my husband and myself.

As I mentioned earlier, people often accuse open-marriage participants of being incredibly or unusually selfish, whereas, at least for me, that couldn't be further from the truth. I have to think about other people all the time in order to make this work—my daughter, my husband, my lovers, their other partners. I have failed at this at times, and small disasters have ensued. But that's taught me that I do have to be particularly conscious, communicative, and honest. I believe it's more selfish to spend one's time obsessing about sex, and that Christopher and I were both worse off prior to opening our marriage, because we spent time thinking about what we didn't have, rather than what we wanted and could get from each other. We felt sorry for ourselves and blamed each other. What is truly selfish, though, is people's thinking their way of life is any better than anyone else's.

Our society has gone crazy around the idea of selfishness. We live in a world that's all about having the most money, having the best body, "having it all," regardless of how you have to get it. Meanwhile, women specifically are told that we can have it all, but we are simultaneously expected to be selfless when it comes to anyone and anything in our lives, from our partners to our children to our colleagues. We are never supposed to put our needs before others'; we need to be good wives and good mothers. We certainly give lip service to having moved beyond this particular paradigm, but we're deluding ourselves if we think we really have.

In her book *Surrendering to Marriage,* the title of which alone gives me the chills, author Iris Krasnow writes, "Surrendering to marriage means we must be forgiving and flexible when what we really feel like doing is spewing venomous remarks. We must give back rubs or our bodies when we feel like reading or sleeping. We must keep our marriages alive, and revive them when they are dying."[9] The book has sold amazingly well. Countless numbers of women have signed on. Countless years of fighting for women's rights have been lost or ignored in the process.

And if you think Krasnow is simply some sort of crackpot, think again. She graduated from Stanford and is a professor of communications at American University. She's appeared on *Oprah,* CNN, the *Today* show, *Good Morning*

America, the CBS *Early Show,* NPR's *All Things Considered,* and *The Hour of Power.* She has a wide platform and an equally broad audience, which makes her message all the more frightening. And make no mistake—the "we" Krasnow is referring to here is us women. Boys will be boys, you know. Women who opt for marriage, however, are choosing to sublimate their personal desires.

I'm sorry, but I can't, won't, and don't accept that because I don't believe it. I spent my entire youth and the early years of my marriage adhering to the "it is what it is" argument. Finally breaking free from that mentality allowed me to explore an altogether different way of living that feels more authentic. Krasnow writes, "When my husband feels pampered, he is more affectionate, more positive about me, about us, about everything. And that sets off a cycle of compassion and loving-kindness and passion that keeps us going around and around. . . . "[10] Wow. Sounds like something straight out of the 1950s. That sort of behavior would make me feel like a slave. *Keep smiling,* I'd tell myself as I picked up his things. *Please, sir, may I have another?* I'd think as I listened to his complaints. *This is a woman's lot,* I'd remind myself as he did as he liked and I accepted and enabled it all. I don't think so.

Yet, amazingly and terrifyingly, this way of thinking is prevalent among wives. Keep your husband happy if you want to have a good marriage. Give up what you want and need. It's all about compromise, the experts say—only it isn't, because behavior doesn't qualify as compromising when the woman is actually doing nothing but sacrificing, while her husband interprets what's going on as their being engaged in some sort of joint giving and accommodating process. Not good. Incredibly bad, actually.

But, come on, who wouldn't want a Krasnow wife? Someone who's always at home, on call, ready to rub your feet or swab the deck or whatever your little heart desires. Sign me up. Only problem is that it's no way to foster partnership and intimacy and all of the things that make a relationship real. Thinking about it in these terms reminds me of the famous 1971 essay written by Judy Syfers (now Judy Brady again after her divorce) for *Ms.* magazine, called "Why I Want a Wife." It's a biting satire that speaks of the utter selflessness that wives are "required" to adopt as they care for husband, children, and home without faltering or thinking for a moment about themselves. They should be working, cooking, cleaning, mothering, doctoring, administrating, organizing, scheduling, ironing, and doing it all without a complaint. "I want a wife who will not bother me with rambling complaints about a wife's duties. But I want a wife who will listen to me. . . . "[11]

While both Krasnow and Syfers write about unequal setups, one writes about it earnestly and the other ironically. Despite the fact that most women profess to want a marriage in which they refuse to be confined to a role, and in which they instead stand up for what they want and need, this is too often not happening in practice, because women naturally want to bend and compromise and nurture and take care of everything. We are still getting the message to embody the selfless, angelic trinity of the wife, the mother, and the eternal virgin.

Ironically, giving ourselves up to marriage often means giving away the best part of us—the part that a partner who truly loves and honors the whole of you should really enjoy. The reason men don't just get a prostitute and a maid is because they want a partnership, just like their wives do. But within Krasnowlike definitions of wife and mother, an equal partnership isn't possible. It's demeaning to both partners and doesn't give the relationship a fighting chance. Owning someone does not work—whether that's about housework or sex. The best marriages are the ones between two complete people, and that takes thinking and understanding and acceptance. And it requires wives' not simply saying, "Yes, dear," and instead voicing their desires and requirements and opinions and feelings—even when there's a cost.

When I got married, I did not agree to shed my selfhood at the altar. I did not agree to grin and bear it. I did not agree to be some sort of lobotomized automaton. Being true to yourself does not make you selfish. Fulfilling your needs does not make you selfish. However, being a martyr and suggesting that your life is better than others' lives because you "suffer" is terribly selfish. *Look at me,* women who sacrifice everything are saying. *I'm a better wife than you.* I'm not buying it, because it's a lousy bill of goods that society has been trying to sell women for way too long. We live in a "me, me, me" world that expects wives to give it all so their husbands can have it all. And we're supposed to suck it up and do it with a smile.

In an essay originally published in *Lear's* magazine in 1993, lifestyle and psychology writer Amy Cunningham demonstrates this very phenomenon, using a woman's smile as a metaphor. In the essay, entitled "Why Women Smile," Cunningham argues that we are required to smile—literally—in order to put others at ease and put our own needs on the back burner. "Smiles are not the small and innocuous things they appear to be: Too many of us smile in lieu of showing what's really on our minds."[12] Just keep smiling, and everything will be all right. It's a frightening enabling technique and a horrifying means of keeping women (read: wives) subjugated.

Cunningham continues, "Evidently, a woman's happy, willing deference is something the world wants visibly demonstrated. Woe to the waitress, personal assistant or receptionist, the flight attendant, or any other woman in the line of public service whose smile is not offered up to the boss or client as proof that there are no storm clouds—no kids to support, no sleep that's being missed—rolling into the sunny workplace landscape."[13] And, I might add, woe to the wife or girlfriend who fails to just keep smiling and instead articulates her needs and desires. A man who does so is standing up for himself; but a woman does so, and she is inherently selfish. This idea seeps insidiously into the way we manage our marriages.

I zealously reject the idea that I'm being "selfish" because I want to be happy, and refuse to plaster a fake permasmile on my face solely to please others. I do understand that, in order to feel better about themselves and their own decisions, some people think they need to characterize others' behavior and choices as selfish. Still, when they're pointing fingers and saying, "You're being selfish," or, "How dare you live your life that way?" I can't help but feel like the truth comes closer to: *Wait—does that mean I could live that way, too? Does that mean I don't have to live the way I'm living?* But these types of questions are too scary and complicated for most people to deal with. It's much easier for them to scapegoat people like me and go on living as they've been living, using the mantra that has gotten them this far: *This is the right way to do things because this is the way things have always been done. She is bad. She is wrong. I am right.* So what's more important—to be happy or right?

Sadly, most people choose the latter because they simply cannot stand the social pressure of doing something that is not perceived as "right." A further complication, of course, is that "right" isn't black or white. And what's right by one person's standards doesn't necessarily ensure even their own happiness. Personally, I would rather be happy and doing what's true for me than striving for someone else's perception of what's right. I'm okay with not knowing how all of this is supposed to work. I'm willing to admit that I don't know, and to check in with my partners and myself about how everyone is feeling as we go. For me, being honest and being allowed to be honest have gotten me to a level of awareness that is as enlightening as I have ever known an experience to be. In turn, my relationship now has an authenticity that it lacked before; this omission was so unchecked that, left unattended much longer, my marriage would likely have disintegrated.

There aren't many things more exhausting than hiding and lying and sneaking around, which is why open marriage is more about being thoughtful than it is about being selfish. Open marriage is the opposite of settling for something; it's about seeking what could be. And, because people are going to ask, yes, it's also about sex. But, as I've said before, I don't believe that makes it any less important than any of the many other issues every couple has to address.

it's hard to gauge what kinds of

couples most people presuppose are in open marriages, but media representations tend toward visions of people living at the very edges of society, whether with a sort of hippie sensibility or a tattoos-and-piercings type of style. There's also a sense that women in open marriages either look like glittery porn stars or opt for housecoats and caftans over

True Religion jeans and ringer T-shirts. Not that there are many depictions in the first place: one couple on *Oprah* in September 2007; four couples on VH1's *Women Seeking Women: A Bi-Curious Journey* in the fall of 2007 (although this series didn't call the marriages "open," I have to imagine that's what audiences will think about them, since this is ultimately a reality show about the pursuit of orgies); and a smattering of people in a number of episodes of HBO's *Real Sex.*

But what about women like me? Where are we? The majority of us may be hiding, perhaps out of fear of being judged or misunderstood. I'm the type of woman who could pass as your next-door neighbor, or the mom you sit next to at PTA meetings. And despite, or maybe because of, how seemingly just like everyone else I am, I am the face of twenty-first-century sex and marriage—with all its nuances and ins and outs. Erase all your mental images of '70s porn stars and late-night cable specials. Bisexuality, open marriage, polyamory, and other living and loving arrangements are often referred to as "alternative," but, given their prevalence, I suggest we start considering how mainstream they actually already are—maybe as prevalent as a Starbucks on a street corner. It's just that Starbucks would never dream of trying to pose as anything other than a coffee shop.

Most people involved in open marriages are honest, open-minded, and intellectual. I am sure there are close-minded people out there, those who think that their way of life is the only way. But for the most part, people who choose open marriage do, in fact, think through the consequences of their actions, and tend to have partners who can wrap their minds around the complexities of love and marriage and the idea of sexuality as a continuum. As opposed to people who are cheating—and therefore, by definition, participating in a dishonest version of an open relationship—those of us who are acknowledging what we're doing are probably more likely to be partnered successfully for years to come. In an August 2007 piece about open marriage for ABC News online, writer Russell Goldman offers insights from author Dossie Easton, who explains that "polyamorous marriages were no more or less successful than monogamous marriages, but at least the polyamorous were never surprised to learn their spouse was cheating."[14]

Open marriage does, of course, have to feel like a viable option for both partners, and if it seems wrong or impossible to handle, then the couple will need to figure out their options: Either dig in and try to make it work, despite the other person's dissatisfaction, or decide to separate. Whether either of these is a happier or better option varies from couple to couple, but in my experience, for an open marriage to succeed, both partners have to open their hearts and minds to what their life is actually going to look like to them, as well as to how it will likely appear to those around them.

"It depends almost entirely on the people involved and their willingness to tell the truth and do the work,"[15] says

Deborah Anapol, psychologist and author of *Polyamory: The New Love Without Limits,* in the same ABC News piece that featured Easton. And that's just it: Christopher and I decided that our love and our marriage were valuable enough for us to want to tell the truth and do what it takes. And so that is what we do—every day—although the meaning of "doing what it takes" can change. But we are ready for and open to change because, well, that's who we are—open. And because being open is so important to us, so is being open about that openness.

I'm tired of being portrayed as something I'm not, of being suspected of getting involved in a kind of relationship that is not representative of the one I'm actually in. It's always frustrating when people make assumptions about you when they know nothing of your experience—but that goes for anything from sexuality to race to education to social class. More troubling to me is that people have such preconceptions because nothing in our culture allows for a broader understanding that plenty of people are thriving in open marriages. Not a single familiar image, in the popular media or elsewhere, portrays a functioning and healthy open marriage. Really, open marriage looks like you and it looks like me. So what I'd like to see, at the very least, is open marriage acknowledged as a better option than cheating. Maybe if practitioners of open marriage were able to stand up and speak to the more common experience of our relationships, we would find the comfort in company that we are all seeking. And with that company would come understanding from those in society who, until then, had been unable to understand and accept this way of life— either for themselves or for others.

In my open marriage, I've focused mostly on allowing myself to flirt a little more than I would have before. I don't know how much flirting is allowed within traditional marriages, but lines tend to be drawn around things like dancing or casual touching with other people, or whether you should mention your marital status right up front. I don't worry about crossing any of those lines now, and that has been probably the most fun, liberating, and surprisingly satisfying thing about being in an open marriage. I feel more alive. It's allowed me to fulfill fantasies that I either couldn't or wouldn't want to act out with my husband, but that I have always wanted to take one step further (though not necessarily all the way to the bedroom). Sometimes—more often than not, actually—these encounters end at flirting and the "what if?" stage. The number of people I've actually gone to that next level with is very small.

Open marriage works for me, and it works well. But I'll be the first to admit it's definitely *not* for everyone. Some people don't want anything other than monogamy. Some people have trust issues. If you can't stop yourself from checking your partner's email or going through his receipts, open marriage is likely going to put you in the loony bin. Some people prefer simplicity over all else, and open marriage is not always cut and dried. It involves thinking and negotiating and being aware. For us, it's worth it. But you have to want it. Or, perhaps, you have to need it. It has to be the way you feel compelled to live.

Open marriage is not for the insecure. It is not for people who are concerned about what the Joneses think, or whose self-worth is inextricably tied to their partners' faithfulness and attention. It is not for people who like things predictable and consistent, because open marriage has neither of those qualities. It is not for the dishonest, the close-minded, the naive, the ignorant, or the incommunicative. It is not for people who are ruled by ego. It is not for the unimaginative or the unadventurous. It's not for everyone, because nothing is for everyone. How many times have you found a good fit in anything labeled one size fits all?

Open marriage is many things, but it is generally not what so many people presume it to be. I am not talking about a free-for-all. I do not want to sleep with everybody all the time. I don't want my entire universe to revolve around "the hunt." I just want to be able to enjoy what piques my interest, instead of having to ignore my desires because I'm married. Being open does not equal being promiscuous, nor does bi or gay or anything else, for that matter. The only thing that equals being promiscuous is promiscuity.

Those involved in open marriages are able to avoid three virtually impossible tasks: having to choose the one and only person they will have (and want to have) sex with for the rest of their lives; promising that their hearts will never decide to love someone else; and predicting who they are going to be five, ten, thirty, or more years from now.

It's easy to summarily dismiss my lifestyle, especially in an effort to elevate one's own life choices. But open marriage is really just a variation on an institution that is desperate for a remodel, a fulfillment of the obvious need for flexibility. Open marriage is not one rigid way of life. Instead, it reflects any number of scenarios, from the arrangement Christopher and I have to living in a commune. It's a matter of making a commitment not to what is, but to what could be. And nothing is more satisfying than a life lived consciously and intentionally. As for others' misconceptions, assumptions, and accusations about my life, well, I'll just say this: We should always remember that no one knows what's going on in anyone else's marriage, and we should never forget that old saying about people who live in glass houses. . . .

Chapter 9
the four
(not-so-easy) steps

As time went on, she realized that several key elements make a successful open marriage, and though those factors involved the community of people she surrounded herself with, it was mostly about how she chose to act and react, and how to be in her relationship and her own skin. Having come this far, she more than realized that it was never going to be easy. She was always going to need to protect her daughter. Things couldn't always be exactly as she wanted them to be. But she was doing it, and she knew she wasn't alone in her journey.

being in a successful open marriage
is about four things: 1) finding the support you need, both within your marriage and from the people around you; 2)

accepting that jealousy is a manufactured emotion that, with enough conscious effort, you can learn to let go of; 3) treating an open marriage as you would a "traditional" one—that is, normalizing it as a choice for everyone; and 4) overcoming people's fears and misunderstanding of open marriage and its supposed consequences on society at large.

Despite the fact that few people who are in open marriages talk about it either publicly (in the media, for example) or openly (that is, within their own community of friends and family members), open marriage—in any number of forms, and going by a variety of alternate names—is becoming more and more common. *Oprah* has featured couples in open marriages, and it's the subject of a variety of new books and articles, from Tristan Taormino's book *Opening Up: Creating and Sustaining Open Relationships* to Em and Lo's article in the June 2007 issue of *Glamour* magazine, "The Secret Sex Lives of American Couples," which featured a couple in an open relationship. In other words, if mass media is any indication, it's increasingly treated as a viable lifestyle choice (though only in more progressive areas, of course).

Unfortunately, I don't live in a particularly forward-thinking part of the country, which means I have to live less openly than I'd like to. That is, although I don't hide the way I live, I don't announce it, either. I introduce my husband as my husband, and my girlfriend as my girlfriend, and answer any questions that might arise. But unless friends and neighbors and colleagues read my work, they might not have any idea about the way I live. We are neither out nor closeted. In a way, it's terrific that it then is no big deal, because why should it be? By the same token, it would be nice to be surrounded constantly by like-minded people with whom I could discuss freely the ins and outs of living openly.

I will say, though, that in certain venues and events, my situation is readily accepted, particularly in the LGBTQ and arts communities. We now know that nonmonogamy has a long, long history; it's just that it hasn't always been referred to as "open marriage." But many people are beginning to see lifelong monogamy for the facade it is. Along with soaring divorce rates, more and more people are defining for themselves what their families will look like, and open relationships are gaining traction.

In my very humble opinion, this has a lot to do with people's wising up. Many thinking men and women find themselves reflecting on why their marriages aren't working, and what marriage might need to look like in order for it *to* succeed. And for those people, who want to retain a relationship they value but that is lacking something, be it large or small, open marriage can be a long-term, happy, and healthy solution. It's the smart way of approaching something that deserves more reliance on logic and less on magic. It takes a heck of a lot more than fairy dust to hold a relationship together.

So, back to the things you need: Number one is support from your spouse. Open marriage is productive only if both partners are onboard. And because the rules can morph and change, it requires ongoing attention and communication. I remember when the need for Christopher and me to support each other, unconditionally, first became abundantly clear to me. It was after our first major "bump," which happened early on with Lisbeth. It was after she decided she no longer wanted to sleep with me, but did want to continue sleeping with Christopher. I specifically asked him not to have sex with her one night, but he did it anyway. I was crushed. His explanation? He thought my request was silly. I was astounded. His behavior showed a blatant disregard for the boundaries we had set. And what's the point of setting boundaries if they're going to be so casually dismissed? Without at least some sort of guidelines, our open marriage simply wasn't going to work.

When I found out that he had specifically ignored my very simple wish, I felt compelled to leave him—not because he'd slept with her, but because he'd betrayed me. My anger and frustration weren't about sex; they were about trust. I reminded him how betrayed he had felt when Grace and I were together, and with that, he was able to see my perspective. He apologized, but I still felt torn. It was obvious that he was genuinely sorry, but I was also incredibly upset. The bottom line was that we were just beginning to navigate how our open marriage was going to operate, and it dawned on me that the only way it could work would be if we caught each other when we stumbled, even if that meant supporting each other in what seemed like unusual ways. I had to juggle being the hurt wife and the friend to the guy who'd hurt his wife. It wasn't easy, but it also turned out to be a very deep way of better knowing someone I already loved.

Because most people consider being in an honest open relationship living alternatively, it's not always easy to get the support you need. I've been lucky enough to find it through the friends and family members I've told, as well as from online communities like Polyamory.org and PracticalPolyamory.com. (You'll find a more complete list of sites and publications in the appendix and the Works Consulted pages of this book.) No one has rejected me because of my choice to open my marriage. I also know that not everyone understands. Through the friendship grapevine, it has gotten back to me that some of my friends can't completely wrap their heads around it, but they have been supportive nonetheless. I believe that's because Christopher's and my friends genuinely care about us, even when they need some help understanding our choices.

People who choose open relationships have to be prepared to stretch a little, too, both to help other people understand and to support one another within the relationship. Sometimes the only person you have to talk to about what's going on is the very person you are having the relationship with, and you can often talk to each other in ways that might not be possible in closed relationships. For example, people in traditional marriages may not be "allowed" to express love or sexual interest, or perhaps any feelings whatsoever, for anyone other than their primary partner. Being closed necessitates hiding. Being open necessitates revelation.

Christopher and I recovered from our first big debacle almost instantly, simply because we decided we would. So much of navigating a new lifestyle involves letting go of the "norms" and "meanings" to which people have grown accustomed. We were figuring things out together, and we had to learn to talk to each other and to listen—not to what we *thought* the other person was saying, but to what they were actually saying. We continue to work at that. Of course, people in monogamous relationships must work at this, too, but because of the intricacies of open marriages and polyamory, being extra communicative becomes, or at least feels, more crucial.

Even though we know that talking is paramount, it's not always easy, especially for Christopher. For example, when things ended with Christopher and Lisbeth and we all went back to being "just friends," it was tough for all of us, as any change is. But Christopher suffered a different kind of loss than either Lisbeth or I did—and, I believe, a more difficult one. She and I fell back into our friendship easily, but he had had no real relationship with her before our sexual one started, and so he was left feeling like an outsider. He had been intimate with her, as physically intimate as any two people can be, and then suddenly he was back to being the husband of her best friend. Period.

"Is this too weird?" he asked me one night as he described his feelings of loss.

"Not at all," I answered. "I'm the only one you really can talk to, and I'm happy to listen." It was an amazing affirmation of our choice to be open, and in terms of communication, the experience provided a bridge of sorts for us. We were talking as we never had before.

Christopher's loss was real, but it was also strange and uncharted in terms of my helping him to work through it. How do you comfort your husband when he has broken up with his lover? The same way you would help anyone else you love survive a difficult time: You listen and love them and appreciate what they are experiencing for what it is. And you don't insert yourself. It would have been easy for me to say, "How can you be so upset if you love me?" or, "What does this say about how you feel about our relationship if you're so worried about losing her?" But *I* had nothing to do with what he was feeling. And seeing him through it—watching him, listening to him, helping him—helped me, once again, to see him as a whole person, and not just as who he was in relation to me. It's a marvelous human and intellectual challenge to think solely of someone else, and to not interject yourself into their particular scenario. It is not something we do often enough. Open marriage and polyamory have given me that opportunity at many turns, but it's not for the faint of heart.

if you do want to give open marriage

a shot, you have to be strong enough to deal with all of the new feelings, problems, and experiences that it might throw at you. You have to know that jealousy is bound to rear its ugly head. This is the second issue on my list, because it's the unfortunate sibling of the supportive lover. It's a dangerous relation, and you'll need to decide what you will do with it when it inevitably arises: allow it to eat you up or make you question yourself and your relationship? Or can you use it as a chance to address why you're feeling jealous in the first place? We feel jealous when we feel insecure, so it's imperative that we examine our relationship's security, or lack thereof, and where it's coming from. Is it you? Is it your partner? Exploring your reasons for feeling jealous can help you gain some perspective on it.

I'm not suggesting this is easy—not by a long shot—but I do believe that it will allow you to see yourself and your partner differently—as individuals, not as wholly defined by each other. And that can result in your creating a space where more love can grow, instead of one in which resentment insinuates itself as it does when jealousy, rather than understanding, is your guide. Not being jealous has to be a conscious choice, and it's a choice I have to work at and remind myself of, one that requires years of deprogramming.

Acknowledging, assessing, and discussing each issue, challenge, and question as it comes up has taught me things about both Christopher and myself that I could not have otherwise learned, and that, to an extent, I did not previously imagine were possible. It's not easy work, but the pleasure is in the challenge. When Socrates was on trial for heresy for prompting students to think for themselves and challenge what they had been told, he responded by telling the court, "The unexamined life is not worth living." I couldn't agree more. It might seem easier, but what's the point? When I started looking at my own life and my marriage was when I figured out how to get to where I wanted to go—that is, how to continue my journey toward having a happy partnership.

even when you do have a relatively easy time transitioning into an open marriage, it's highly unlikely that everyone around you will see your choice as something they understand, or even consider legitimate, either socially or romantically. Despite having my family's and close friends' backing, I have had plenty of experience with people whose responses to my lifestyle have been anything *but* supportive. These include being aggressive, condescending, and just plain mean-spirited. As I mentioned earlier, people who see open marriage as deviant feel perfectly comfortable labeling me a whore. It makes it easier for them to rationalize and compartmentalize my life. Thinking of me as a bad person and a bad wife and a bad mother is convenient and facilitates their separating themselves from me. Otherwise, they could be just like me. And that's simply too scary a proposition to address. The best thing I can do for myself, then, as well as for others who choose to live in open relationships, is to own being open, and to respect it as I would any more traditional arrangement. Normalizing open marriage among its participants is the first step toward gaining acceptance in the community at large.

For me, it's not so important to meet the standards that other people impose upon me as it is to be able to live in harmony with my neighbors and friends and acquaintances, particularly where Emily is concerned.

The scenario I fear most—which, thank goodness, hasn't happened and I pray never will—is that people will stop letting their children come over to our house to play with our daughter. One of my very closest friends, Alex, ended up taking issue with my lifestyle at one point in our friendship. She was worried that her children might "see something" when they were playing at our house. She felt unnerved by my own comfort with my open relationship, and because she and her husband and I had experimented a bit together at one point, she lashed out at me, rather than talking through her reasons for feeling upset or regretting her choice, or whatever the issue was for her. I respect my partners' privacy just as I expect them to honor mine, but other people can be unpredictable, to be sure, and that is one of the greatest hazards of being in an open relationship. That risk can require significant management, and it cannot always be controlled.

Alex and I ended up having a long talk and working out our problems, though I don't know that we ever quite got to the root of her discomfort. The problem stemmed from her not being able to wrap her head around what had happened. There was no tidy little box into which she could fit our liaison—or me, for that matter. I had no problem with what had happened with Alex and her husband, and I didn't want us or our children to lose out on the friendships that were at stake. But without the box, she questioned her own acceptance of me.

It's sad when we question our own judgment, our own gut instincts, because they don't mirror what everyone else is saying or doing or believing. Making an open marriage effective means being prepared to work through any rough spots with your friends, surrounding yourself with as many enlightened people as you can, and setting an example for people of just how normal and reasonable an open marriage can be. I feel like I'm finally at a pretty good point with most of my close friends, but there's always the potential for missteps with them, and then there are the issues that arise when I meet new people or acknowledge my circumstances to current acquaintances, particularly people I know through Emily's school. It's a calculated risk. But I can think of few things in life worth doing that aren't.

Things are different for me now because Jemma is the only person I see outside of my marriage. Without doing a lot of dating and having various relationships, I have less potential for turmoil, to be sure. But it's still hard to juggle. I want to be with Emily and Jemma and Christopher all the time, yet I can't because Jemma doesn't live with us. And that makes me sad sometimes. When I think about it in the simplest of terms, our arrangement feels like a forced, contrived, and unnecessary separation of people who, outside of social conventions, would likely live together. The idea of living with my family and Jemma has certainly occurred to me, but that's not something any of us want, at least not for now.

This has to do with where I live, my desire to protect my daughter, and the fact that our society cares too much about how people love. And so, despite my comfort and my openness, and despite living alternatively and following my heart in my relationships, I still, in many ways, live under the thumb of others' expectations and ideals. That will likely continue as long as Emily lives at home, because I want to protect her from other people's ignorance and potential wrath.

What an awful commentary—that because I enjoy sex, particularly in a way that too many people find abnormal, I'm automatically deemed mentally ill or unstable or dangerous to my own child. In an incredibly unscientific survey, I gave questionnaires to people in open relationships, and asked them about the hows and whys of their daily lives. One respondent, whom I'll call Sara, expressed fears that were all too familiar to me. "We do not look like the ideal family, so it would be easy for people to take that next step to the idea that there is something wrong with us as parents."

the final stage in figuring out how to be in a successful open marriage is overcoming our own worries and other people's misunderstandings about how we define our relationships. There's nothing unusual about people who choose open marriage, except perhaps that we opt to tell the truth to ourselves and to one another. There wouldn't be any great apocalyptic end to life as we know it if the "accepted" definition of a marriage or a relationship or even a family were to include those of us who don't look like a family straight out of *Leave It to Beaver.* Open marriage does not and will not disrupt life as we now know it. It already *is* life as we know it, even though some people pretend not to understand that. They seem terrified of open marriages, of any alternative lifestyle, for the same reason that they're scared of anything unknown: They don't know what to expect around the corner. This situation is similar, and not surprisingly so, to society's struggle with interracial marriage and its continued wrangling with same-sex marriage. My hope is that others will come clean about their lifestyles, as I have, as we work toward creating a society where people in heterosexual, monogamous marriages are not the only ones who are permitted to live free from harsh and unfounded judgment.

I'm not out to change anyone. I'm interested in changing how we look at everyone. Everyone needs support. No one needs jealousy and no one benefits from it. Open marriage is happening all around us. And no walls are going to come tumbling down because of it. Living openly is about living honestly, loving fully, and being able to embrace that choice freely. This is what I want for myself and others, both those who are already living in open marriages and those who are interested in exploring its possibilities.

Chapter 10

our very own
happily ever after

She finally decided that she didn't need to know what it all meant or where it was all going. What she did know was that everyone is different, so it made sense to her that every marriage might be different. For now, her marriage was working. She had a husband and a girlfriend who loved her, and a daughter who was doing just fine. Why shouldn't they keep on doing what they were doing, she reasoned, and see if they couldn't define for themselves their own happily ever after?

after doing lots of research, talking with nearly everyone I knew, and having all kinds of experiences that I'd longed to have, I came to terms with the fact that I was okay with not having it all figured out, and not knowing for sure why living in an open marriage is the best choice for me. And I still don't know why, no matter how much I want to have it all figured out. What I do know is that people are all different, marriages are different, and my husband, my girlfriend, and I—and Emily—are happy.

I know from my experience that following my instincts and acting on what feels right are the keys to living an authentic life. Going against my gut simply wasn't working for me. And I've discovered, from talking to countless people about my own experiences, that I am not alone in my thoughts and ideas, or even my practices. Open marriage is not a radical or singular act, which is what I thought it was when I first started down this path. It's far more prevalent than people think, and current trends suggest it will likely become only more commonplace. One need only look at people in their twenties and thirties to see how true that is: They are far more accepting—of gender, sexual preferences, you name it—than previous generations, probably because they've lived among people who have all sorts of arrangements, and because they question everything and accept themselves for who they are. Every generation wants a chance to prove what they can offer. Young people today certainly seem more poised to accomplish that goal than my generation was, let alone those that came before me. This isn't across the board, of course—nothing ever is—but so many of them are seeking to find their own truths, rather than simply following the road map that has been set before them, one that has led so many people down the paths of failed relationships, disillusionment, and dissatisfaction.

My dad used to tell me that when people insist that they know best and ridicule others for their behavior and choices, it's because they're insecure about their own behavior and choices. It wasn't until I was well into adulthood and my marriage, though, that I was able to fully grasp how vital it is to stop listening to other people's assertions that "you just can't do that" or "it's not done that way." I had to find out for myself, and definitely through trial and error, that when it comes to sex and love and relationships, the closed-off, boxed-up, reined-in way I was trying to live wasn't going to work.

For better or worse, people change. When two people in their twenties get married with certain ideals and expectations in mind, it is all but inevitable that they are going to find themselves surprised by what they discover once they have a few years of marriage under their belts. Open marriage and polyamory are just two examples of alternative ways of doing relationships that make space for that change. Hell, they don't just make space for it—they welcome it, breed it. Open marriage, polyamory, and other lifestyles outside of heterosexual, monogamous marriage exist because a lot of people want to reach a different potential where sex and love are concerned, a possibility that traditional marriage bars because of its limiting construct.

Whether or not you personally like these concepts is beside the point. Living openly might not be right for you. It might not even appeal to you. But no matter what your lifestyle preferences are, surely it's time to accept the fact that these more open styles of living do benefit some people, and that it's time to stop ignoring what's going on all around us. More likely than not, if you have kids, they are already spending time in households where the parents are in situations that exist outside of what we have come to call the "norm"—whether they're gay, swinging, or poly. You may be aware of their choices, or you may not, but shouldn't you base your feelings about people on whether you trust them with your children, or whether you'd like to invite them to your home for dinner? Are you honestly any safer believing that no one you know lives differently than you? Does sameness equal safety? The usual saying is that ignorance equals bliss. I say ignorance equals intolerance.

Divorce rates continue to be high, and infidelity becomes a more prevalent issue by the day. If you think that no one you know is cheating on their significant other, think again. There might not be a crimson vowel emblazoned on his or her chest, but that doesn't mean it's not going on right under your nose. In my research, I came across this headline in the August 9, 1854, edition of *The New York Times:* "Growth of Infidelity in the United States." The article read, "It is generally admitted that Infidelity, within the last twenty-five years, has increased in the United States. There are not statistics, so far as we know, on the subject, but the fact itself is too obvious to admit doubt."[1] Some things never change. What does it say about our society that we refuse to face the reality of just how unsuccessful our most common social construct is? How evolved and intelligent is that? Do you think Bill Gates would continue to employ a manufacturing or programming process with a track record as lousy as marriage's? Don't kid yourself.

More and more people are choosing never to get married at all. We're beginning to drown in the negative effects of pursuing a lifestyle that doesn't suit the majority of people. That's not to say that someone can't choose monogamy, but that's what it is—a choice—and precisely what it should remain. Furthermore, it should also be one choice among many, and that means that polyamory should be one of the other options. It's far from new or revolutionary, this idea that we can love more than one person at a time. People are living in intentional communities, in groups of three or four or more, or in separate houses from their spouses while still maintaining happy marriages. Someone who is polyamorous may not be committed to one primary, long-term partner, but may instead see a loose circle of people that rotates and changes. Some people practice polyfidelity, meaning they are involved with and committed to a specific group of people (in any number). But the most common scenario is the triad, or triple, in which three people are committed to one another and may or may not all be sexually involved with one another. What all three people do share is love and respect.

Polyamory is about how love would look outside of any social constructs. Think about it: If no one ever told you how you were "supposed" to do it, whom would you love? How would you love? How many would you love? What would your sexuality look like if no one had prescribed it for you from the moment you were born? These questions may lead you to consider whom you want to share yourself with, and in what way, without being concerned with an arbitrary framework. The only rule in open marriage and/or polyamory is that everyone involved follows the rules—and the rules are set by those involved. It isn't simply a matter of doing whatever you want, with whomever you want, whenever you want. Polyamory is about thinking for yourself. Doing what everyone else is doing because everyone else is doing it is easy. It is seeing beyond that requires far more vision.

my own venture into open marriage

is ongoing. But at this point in my journey, what strikes me as most intriguing is the fact that I knew, from very early on, that traditional marriage wasn't compatible with me. I was always interested in "and," rather than "either/or," and I was never sure that love offered any guarantees. And yet I dove headfirst into marriage. Why? I thought that being committed and doing the thing I was supposed to do would help me come to my senses, but even early on in

my marriage, I realized that love is a state, and a constantly
fluctuating one at that. It is affected by changes in ourselves,
our partners, and the world at large. So when the black-and-
white options we're presented with look like a huge splotch
of gray, what are we to do? We must understand and accept
that we don't have to live within the confines and rules that
society presents for us as "the only way." We have a right to
find our own happiness and our own truth.

Love and sex, much to the discontentment of so
many who believe in happily ever after, are not constant
companions. And those who believe they are will likely
run into disappointment somewhere along the way. It's an
ideal that sets us up for all kinds of falls. Most of us have
had a number of partners by the time we get to that point,
and any of those people may have offered qualities that we
sought or wanted in a significant other. Yet suddenly there
we are, bound to one person for the rest of our lives. Part
of being sexually free prior to marriage, assuming that we
aren't saving ourselves for The One, involves going through
a period of sexual exploration and, if you're lucky, sexual
enlightenment. All of which, again, is considered valid, even
good, by modern standards.

Young women today are generally encouraged to
explore, to find themselves, to be sexually open, but then are
expected to somehow simply shut down as individuals when
they get married and "settle down." But they don't *actually,
naturally* shut down. They simply have an enforced response

because of social conditioning, which demands that we stop being people and start being wives. And so one-night stands and casual sex are socially acceptable at certain points in our lives—college, certainly, and afterwards, as long as we're not married—and then, all of a sudden, sex isn't "just sex" anymore once two people commit to each other. As a result, we are left with an entire society of people trying to conform to an extremely recent social dictate. Truth be told, it's amazing that we aren't failing even more than we already are.

When I tell people I'm in an open relationship, they often ask, "Then why are you even married?" My response: "Why wouldn't we be?" Christopher and I are a good match. Our personalities balance each other out, and we're great coparents. What I've come to realize is that this question stems from a belief, albeit subconscious for many people, that marriage is about sexual ownership. So for those who want further explanation, I sometimes offer this: "We're still married because we believe in traditional marriage based on trust and commitment, not on fireworks or romantic love or sex. We base our other relationships on romance and sex, and our primary one on a much bigger, more long-term picture."

Some people want to know why, given the fact that I've striven to be in an open marriage and have made lots of sacrifices to do so, I have chosen Jemma as my sole partner outside of my marriage. That answer is more complex. I've explained much of it throughout this book—I had had my fill of more casual sexual liaisons; I wanted to be with a woman; I wanted to be with someone whom I really was interested in and cared for; and I wanted something that involved a sense of longevity and commitment.

But when it comes down to it, I can't say whether I'd be with Jemma if I were dating her with the end goal of marriage in mind. She's not sure she wants to live in a household with children, for one. She's younger than I am, and perhaps she'll want to date more people before she decides to settle down—that is, if she decides to settle down at all. She might want to be with someone closer to her age, or a man. And then there are more pragmatic issues: I'm not sure managing a household together would work.

While these might all be reasons not to marry her, or even make a long-term commitment to her, none of them are reasons for not loving her or sleeping with her. So, while I've made it abundantly clear that I don't believe in monogamy, I do believe in committed nonmonogamous relationships. I do believe in responsible nonmonogamy. I do believe that we are intelligent creatures, intelligent enough to have relationships that differ from the modern marriage model. If people can decide to be monogamous, so too can they choose to keep their jealousy and egos in check, and not allow nonmonogamy to turn into promiscuity.

I encourage everyone to set aside all this defining for a moment and simply love a little more. Stretch a bit. Maybe for you, this isn't about finding love outside your marriage.

Maybe it's about sex, or maybe it's the reverse. Or, hell, if your marriage is working for you as is, then maybe open marriage isn't about you in any way at all. But it is—because even though open marriage may not interest you for your own relationship, it does interest others. And my hope is that anyone reading this book will accept those of us for whom finding love beyond our marriages is rewarding. On the other hand, if you *have* found yourself reflected in this book's stories and ideas, consider not beating yourself up. Perhaps you're surprised to discover that this book has affected you in complicated and far-reaching ways, or in ways that feel, quite frankly, like a long-awaited relief.

Just know that being open is about love. And there should never be any restrictions on love. Open marriage stems from a number of different scenarios and relationship dynamics. It can be about anything, take any shape, as long as the people involved are all on the same page. There is no wrong way to do this, other than lying to yourself and your partners, in which case you're no longer talking about being open—and society has all kinds of "acceptable" ways of dealing with that.

I don't think people should ever have to be ashamed of whom and how they love. I can think of plenty of things that are shameful: being cruel to animals, or intentionally hurting someone, or stealing something. But love shouldn't ever be one of these things. I love the man who stands by me always, the man who is the father of my child. And I love the woman who provides me with the kind of emotional support and sexual satisfaction that I don't believe any man or any traditional marriage could give me. What if the problem is not with wanting what we want, but rather with the way we are made to feel for wanting it?

i'd like to see open marriages be as

accepted as closed ones. I'd like to see the term used to refer to a type of relationship that is one of any number of other choices. I'd like "open marriage" to be a commonly used, commonly acknowledged description of a healthy lifestyle, rather than a reference to something that is somehow deviant, perverse, or even unusual. I want people to acknowledge the fact that open marriage represents the state some marriages already exist in (the difference being that adultery means sex with lying, cheating, and sneaking around, while open marriage means sex with all of your cards in view). I personally prefer to know the cards I'm dealing with.

My truth is this: My husband and I got married because we loved and respected each other. We were both looking for the security and stability a marriage provides. We had complementary interests and abilities. We wanted the same things, and each of us had what the other needed to make those things possible. There were sparks at the beginning, of course. We never would have gotten together in the first place if there hadn't been. But once the thrill of early sex faded, I started to feel like a failure. However, I shouldn't have. We had accomplished exactly what we had set out to: We had a house and a child and careers, and we enjoyed each other. So when I sensed a hole because I was lacking passion and fiery sex and desire, I had to realign my thinking. I had to find what was missing and incorporate that into a new version of the marriage I was in, rather than simply expect it to magically come from the partner I had chosen to spend my life with.

And I found what I was looking for—first with a series of male lovers, and now with a committed girlfriend. So I'm married, and I'm honest, and I'm doing what I need to do to create a space in which Christopher and I can continue growing together in our relationship. And our partnership is one that's rooted soundly in the historical tradition of marriage, one founded on building and living a life together, and not solely on the fleeting state of romance. The only difference is that my husband and I reject the suggestion that commitment to each other means signing over our bodies and our hearts. We share those things—with each other and with those whom we bring into our lives. Marriage should not be a prison. It should be a home base from which we can reach out to find those people and those things that can complete us—and our lives.

don't feel sorry for me or my husband.

Please. We don't have a marriage that's lacking; we have it

all. My only regret is not having entered into our marriage with the intention of having this lifestyle from the very beginning. It would have made our current situation easier, since the transition wasn't—and still isn't—a breeze. But it's clear to me how much sense this makes for us, and how little sense it makes to have a one-size-fits-all guideline regarding marriage.

If you do find the combination of factors that allows you to have a great, long-lasting monogamous relationship, good on you. But you're the exception, not the rule. And if you relate to any of the issues that were pulling at me, or have questions about the state of your relationship, don't for one second consider yourself or your marriage a failure. This entire discussion is about looking at marriage—and love and sex, for that matter—in a different way. Some people will reach out to find sex; others, love; still others, both. No matter what someone is looking for, though, conducting that search within the safe and honest realm of an open marriage means that it can be a happy quest and a joyful finding, instead of a guilt-laden path of deception and fear.

My marriage with Christopher and my relationship with Jemma are anything but mutually exclusive. They are perfect together. Perfect. He is my rock and she is my sky. Never would we presume earth and air could fulfill our lives' differing needs in identical ways, and never would we expect to be able to live without one or the other. The same should be true of the people in our lives: Different people fulfill different wants and needs. It's not that complicated.

I'm fearful of where we might end up if we don't open ourselves up. People aren't going to stop having affairs. Gays and lesbians aren't going to become heterosexual. Couples will continue to split up. People will continue to seek out alternative paths, particularly in the aftermath of relationships that have left them stifled and unhappy. What do we want our world to look like? Do we want it dictated by fear and lack of understanding, or do we want it run with experiential wisdom and respect for the truth? Are we willing to open our eyes and open our lives and begin to proactively define for ourselves our personal visions for the future? I already have, and happily ever after has never looked so good.

christopher's
afterword

readers of this book will undoubtedly
form an opinion of me, ranging from flattering to downright
contemptuous. I also envision another camp that suspects
this story is fiction, and that I do not in fact exist at all. My
purpose with this letter is not to influence these preformed
opinions, but rather to provide a voice of support for Jenny.
I admire the audacity and courage my wife has shown
in opening up her most intimate feelings and desires to
complete strangers. I want to thank her for respecting my
feelings by making our experiences, rather than me, the
focal point of her book.

Our relationship—that is, our marriage—has been an
evolution, and I must admit that we have sailed into waters

that I did not imagine when we exchanged vows ten years ago. That does not mean that I love Jenny any less today than I did those many years ago. In fact, it sounds cliché, but it's true nonetheless: My love for her has grown exponentially in this time. The path we have taken is not for everybody, and we do not intend to be role models for alternative lifestyles. I believe our marriage is unique, as is everyone else's. A marriage is a bond between two individuals. When it's successful, each person plays an equal and instrumental part in creating something that neither could even aspire to on their own. What we have is ours, something that we have created together. Our journey is not done by a long shot, for we still have much to learn and experience together. I am blessed to have found a life partner who is sexy, beautiful, loving, and intelligent. She is every bit my equal, as I am hers. If the next chapter of our marriage is half as thrilling and adventuresome as the first, then I will be a happy and contented man.

Respectfully,
Christopher

notes

Chapter 1. What's a Girl to Do?

1. Jessica Valenti, *Full Frontal Feminism: A Young Woman's Guide to Why Feminism Matters* (Emeryville, CA: Seal Press, 2007), 49.

2. Laura Kipnis, *Against Love: A Polemic* (New York: Vintage Books, 2003), 11.

3. *Glamour,* "What's Sexy, What's Scary in Bed," September 2007, 222.

4. Laura Sessions Stepp, "Cupid's Broken Arrow," *Washington Post,* May 7, 2006, D01.

5. Sharon Jayson, "Married Women Unite! Husbands Do Less Housework," *USA Today,* August 29, 2007, 7D.

6. Stephanie Coontz, *Marriage, A History: How Love Conquered Marriage* (New York: Penguin Books, 2005), 311.

Chapter 2. My Orgasm, My Self

1. Helen Fisher, PhD, *Anatomy of Love: A Natural History of Mating, Marriage, and Why We Stray* (New York: Random House, 1992), 86.

2. Alfred C. Kinsey, Wardell B. Pomeroy, and Clyde E. Martin, *Sexual Behavior in the Human Male* (Philadelphia: W. B. Saunders Co., 1948), 409.

3. Nena O'Neill and George O'Neill, *Open Marriage: A New Life Style for Couples* (New York: Avon Books, 1972), 236.

4. Ibid., 237.

5. David P. Barash, PhD, and Judith Eve Lipton, MD, *The Myth of Monogamy: Fidelity and Infidelity in Animals and People* (New York: Henry Holt and Company, 2001), 21.

6. Nena O'Neill and George O'Neill, *Open Marriage,* 254.

7. Hilda Hutcherson, MD, "10 Sex Questions Every Woman Should Ask Herself," *Glamour* magazine, September 2007, 385.

8. E. J. Graff, *What Is Marriage For?* (Boston: Beacon Press, 1999), 35.

9. Susan Faludi, *Backlash* (New York: Crown Publishers, 1991), 160–61.

10. Ibid., 161.

11. Graff, *What Is Marriage For?,* 98

12. Ibid., 96.

13. Barash and Lipton, *The Myth of Monogamy,* 2, 4.

14. Ibid., 1.

15. bell hooks, "Subversive Desire," *Ms.* magazine, April/May 1999, 58.

16. Fisher, *Anatomy of Love,* 76.

17. Kipnis, *Against Love,* 188.

18. Jennifer Baumgardner, "Why more girls are dating . . . girls," *Glamour,* March 2007, 174.

19. Anne Kingston, *The Meaning of Wife* (New York: Farrar, Straus and Giroux, 2004), 7.

Chapter 3. Just Pick Someone Already

1. Fisher, *Anatomy of Love,* 163.

2. Valenti, *Full Frontal Feminism,* 211.

3. Anne Kingston, *The Meaning of Wife* (New York: Farrar, Straus and Giroux, 2004), 117.

4. Kipnis, *Against Love,* 18.

5. Carol Lloyd, "I want you so bad: Now that our president has confessed to adultery, will the American people follow him to the pillory?" Salon.com, August 26, 1998.

6. Iris Krasnow, *Surrendering to Marriage* (New York: Hyperion Books, 2002), 140.

7. Ibid., 23.

Chapter 4. Everyone Else Manages to Do It, Why Can't I?

1. Fisher, *Anatomy of Love,* 298.

2. Barash and Lipton, *The Myth of Monogamy,* 2.

3. Barash, "Deflating the Myth of Monogamy," *Chronicle of Higher Education,* April 20, 2001, B16–17.

4. Ker Than, "Scientists Study Factors Behind Fidelity," MSNBC, November 20, 2006, www.msnbc.msn.com.

5. Stephanie Coontz, *Marriage, a History: How Love Conquered Marriage* (New York: Penguin Books, 2005), 6.

6. Ibid., 7.

7. Kipnis, *Against Love,* 60.

8. Ibid., 61.

9. Peggy Vaughan, "Who Has Affairs—and Why," DearPeggy.com, www.dearpeggy.com/affairs.html.

10. Ibid.

11. Stephany Alexander, "Cheating and Infidelity Statistics: Are Men Cheating More Than Women?" WomanSavers.com, www.womansavers.com/Cheating-Infidelity-statistics.asp.

12. Alexander, "Sex and Relationship Polls," WomanSavers.com, www.womansavers.com/relationship-polls.asp.

13. Baumgardner, *Look Both Ways: Bisexual Politics* (New York: Farrar, Straus and Giroux, 2007), 78.

14. Kinsey and others, *Sexual Behavior in the Human Male;* Kinsey and others, *Sexual Behavior in the Human Female* (Philadelphia: W. B. Saunders Co., 1953).

Chapter 5. This Is a Test

1. Polyamorous Percolations, September 21, 2007, www.polyinthemedia.blogspot.com.

2. Michelle Chihara, "Multi-Player Option: Young polyamorists are rewriting the laws of desire," Nerve.com, June 8, 2004, www.nerve.com/dispatches/multiplayeroption.

3. Ibid.

Chapter 6. Having Our Cake and Eating It, Too

1. Kipnis, *Against Love,* 132.

2. Dossie Easton and Catherine A. Liszt, *The Ethical Slut: A Guide to Infinite Sexual Possibilities* (San Francisco: Greenery Press, 1997), 23.

3. Jenny Block, "Portrait of an Open Marriage: Jenny Block reveals an unconventional marriage arrangement that worked," TangoMag. com, November 28, 2006, www.tangomag.com.

4. Block, "Portrait of an Open Marriage," HuffingtonPost.com, November 28, 2006, www.huffingtonpost.com/jenny-block.

5. Patrick Carnes, PhD, "Contrary to Love: Helping the Sexual Addict" (Minneapolis: CompCare Publishers, 1989), 5–6.

6. Annie Sprinkle, "Sex Addiction," AnnieSprinkle.org, www.annie sprinkle.org/html/writings.

7. Block, "Portrait of an Open Marriage."

8. Ibid.

9. Stephen A. Mitchell, *Can Love Last?* (New York: W. W. Norton & Company, 2002), 104.

10. Graff, *What Is Marriage For?*, 82.

11. Ibid., 103.

Chapter 7. You Can't Run Out of Love

1. Lisa Diamond, "Development of sexual orientation among adolescent and young adult women," *Developmental Psychology* 34 (1998): 1,085–95.

2. Diamond, *Sexual Fluidity* (Cambridge, MA: Harvard University Press, 2008). This information is compiled from reviews and descriptions from Harvard University Press and Amazon.com, www.hup. harvard.edu and www.amazon.com.

3. Baumgardner, *Look Both Ways,* 10.

4. Jeannine DeLombard, "Femmenism," in *To Be Real,* ed. Rebecca Walker (New York: Anchor Books, 1995), 28.

5. Ibid.

6. Baumgardner, *Look Both Ways,* 170.

7. Ibid., 50.

8. Kinsey, *Sexual Behavior in the Human Male,* 639.

Chapter 8. It's Not Necessarily What You Think

1. Olive Skene Johnson, PhD, *The Sexual Spectrum: Why We're All Different* (Vancouver: Raincoast Books, 2004), 214.

2. Bernard Gert, "The Definition of Morality," in *The Stanford University Encyclopedia of Philosophy* (fall 2005 edition), ed. Edward N. Zalta, http://plato.stanford.edu/archives/fall2005.

3. Easton and Liszt, *The Ethical Slut,* 4.

4. Albert Einstein, "Religion and Science," *New York Times Magazine,* November 9, 1930.

5. Easton and Liszt, *The Ethical Slut,* 4.

6. Miriam Axel Lute, "And Baby Makes Four: My daughter has two moms, one dad, and no complaints," Babble.com, www.babble.com.

7. Ibid.

8. Ibid.

9. Krasnow, *Surrendering to Marriage,* 13.

10. Ibid., 174.

11. Judy Syfers, "Why I Want a Wife," *Ms.* magazine, spring 1972, 144.

12. Amy Cunningham, "Why Women Smile," in *The Writer's Presence* (New York: Bedford/St. Martin's, 2003), 336.

13. Ibid., 337.

14. Russell Goldman, "Are Open Marriages More Successful Than Traditional Couplings? A New Generation Tries Swinging, but Leaves the Leisure Suits in the Closet," ABC News, August 10, 2007, www.abcnews.go.com/US/LifeStages.

15. Deborah Anapol, ABC News, August 10, 2007, www.abcnews. go.com/US/LifeStages.

Chapter 10. Our Very Own Happily Ever After

1. "Growth of Infidelity in the United States," *New York Times,* August 9, 1854.

works consulted

Abichandani, Jaishri. 1999. Sleeping arrangements. *Ms.* magazine, April/May, www.msmagazine.com.

Alexander Stephany. "Cheating and Infidelity Statistics: Are Men Cheating More Than Women?" WomanSavers.com, www.woman savers.com/Cheating-Infidelity-statistics.asp.

Anapol, Deborah. 1997. *Polyamory: The New Love Without Limits.* San Rafael, CA: IntiNet Resource Center.

Barash, David P., PhD. Deflating the myth of monogamy. Trinity University, www.trinity.edu/rnadeau.

Barash, David P., PhD, and Judith Eve Lipton, MD. 2001. *The Myth of Monogamy.* New York: Henry Holt and Company.

Barker, Kenneth L., ed. 1995. *The NIV Study Bible.* Grand Rapids, MI: The Zondervan Corporation.

Baumgardner, Jennifer. 2007. Why more girls are dating . . . girls. *Glamour,* March, 174–75.

———. 2007. *Look Both Ways: The Politics of Bisexuality.* New York: Farrar, Straus and Giroux.

Belle, Jennifer. 1999. Yesterday taking the subway, I cried. *Ms.* magazine, April/May, www.msmagazine.com.

Begley, Sharon. 2007. The truths we want to deny. *Newsweek,* 21 May, 58.

Bhattacharya, Sanjiv. Interview with Hugh Hefner. Men.style.com, http://men.style.com/details.

Block, Jenny. 2006. "Portrait of an Open Marriage: Jenny Block reveals an unconventional marriage arrangement that worked," Tango magazine, 28 November, www.tangomag.com.

Blume, Judy. 1975. *Forever.* New York: Pocket Books.

Boyd, Blanch McCrary. 1999. Adultery is not a problem for lesbians because we don't have sex. *Ms.* magazine, April/May, www.ms magazine.com.

Bright, Susie. 1995. *Sexwise: America's Favorite X-Rated Intellectual Does Dan Quayle, Catharine MacKinnon, Stephen King, Camille Paglia, Nicholson Baker, Madonna, the Black Panthers and the GOP.* Pittsburgh, PA: Cleis Press.

Brzezinski, Mika. 2005. Double trouble. CBS News, 13 February, www.cbsnews.com.

Bussel, Rachel Kramer. 2006. Keeping married sex hot. *Village Voice,* 30 August–5 September, 124.

———. 2005. Whore pride. *Village Voice,* 13 January.

Carnes, Patrick, PhD. 1989. "Contrary to Love: Helping the Sexual Addict." Minneapolis: CompCare Publishers.

Carson, Anne. 1986. *Eros: The Bittersweet.* Princeton, NJ: Princeton University Press.

Chihara, Michelle. 2004. Multi-player option: Young polyamorists are rewriting the laws of desire. Nerve.com, 8 June, www.nerve.com/dispatches/multiplayeroption.

Coontz, Stephanie. 2005. *Marriage, a History: How Love Conquered Marriage.* New York: Penguin Books.

Cunningham, Amy. 2003. "Why Women Smile," in The Writer's Presence. New York: Bedford/St. Martin's.

Davis, Shannon N., Theodore N. Greenstein, and Jennifer P. Gerteisen Marks. 2007. Effects of Union Type on Division of Household Labor: Do Cohabiting Men Really Perform More Housework? Journal of Family Issues 28: 1246–72.

DeLombard, Jeannine. 1995. Femmenism. *To Be Real.* New York: Anchor Books.

Demetriou, Danielle. 2006. Open relationships: One lover is never enough. *Independent,* 11 June.

de Waal, Frans B. M. 1995. Bonobo sex and society. *Scientific American,* March, 82–88.

Diamond, L. M. 1998. Development of sexual orientation among adolescent and young adult women. *Developmental Psychology* 34:1085–95.

———. 2003. Was it a phase? Young women's relinquishment of lesbian/bisexual identities over a 5-year period. *Journal of Personality and Social Psychology* 84, no. 2:352–64.

———. 2003. What does sexual orientation orient? A behavioral model distinguishing romantic love and sexual desire. *Psychological Review* 110, no. 1:173–92.

———. 2005. A new view of lesbian subtypes: Stable vs. fluid identity trajectories over an 8-year period. *Psychology of Women Quarterly* 29:119–28.

———. 2007. A dynamical systems approach to the development and expression of female same-sex sexuality. *Perspectives on Psychological Science* 2, no. 2:142–61.

Einstein, Albert. 1930. Religion and Science, New York Times Magazine, 9 November.

Easton, Dossie and Catherine A Liszt. 1997. *The Ethical Slut: A Guide to Infinite Sexual Possibilities.* San Francisco: Greenery Press.

Em and Lo. 2007. The secret sex lives of American couples. *Glamour,* June, 266–69.

———. 2005. The new monogamy. *New York* magazine, 12 November, www.nymag.com.

Emin, Tracey. 2007. A pop romance. *Independent,* 14 February, 3–5.

Esterhazy, Louise. 2007. A little hanky-panky. *W* magazine, September, 640.

Faderman, Lillian. 1991. *Odd Girls and Twilight Lovers: A History of Lesbian Life in Twentieth-Century America.* New York: Penguin Books.

Faludi, Susan. 1991. *Backlash*. New York: Crown Publishers.

Fisher, Helen, PhD. 1992. *Anatomy of Love: A Natural History of Mating, Marriage, and Why We Stray*. New York: Random House.

Gert, Bernard. 2005. The Definition of Morality. In The Stanford Encyclopedia of Philosophy, http://plato.stanford.edu/archives/fall2005.

Glamour. 2007. What's sexy, what's scary in bed, September, 222.

Goldman, Russell. 2007. Are open marriages more successful than traditional couplings? A new generation tries swinging, but leaves the leisure suits in the closet. ABC News, 12 August, www.abcnews.go.com.

Graff, E. J. 1999. *What Is Marriage For?* Boston: Beacon Press.

Hanauer, Cathi, ed. 2002. *The Bitch in the House: 26 Women Tell the Truth About Sex, Solitude, Work, Motherhood, and Marriage*. New York: HarperCollins.

Harris, Paul. 2005. Forget monogamy and swinging. We're seriously polyamorous. *Observer*, 13 November.

Hite, Shere. 1976. *The Hite Report*. New York: Seven Stories Press.

hooks, bell. 1999. Subversive desire. *Ms.* magazine, April/May, www. msmagazine.com.

Hilda Hutcherson, MD. 2007. 10 Sex Questions Every Woman Should Ask Herself, Glamour, September.

Janus, Samuel S., PhD, and Cynthia L. Janus, MD. 1993. *The Janus Report on Sexual Behavior.* New York: John Wiley & Sons, Inc.

Johnson, Olive Skene, PhD. 2004. *The Sexual Spectrum: Why We're All Different.* Vancouver: Raincoast Books.

Kingston, Anne. 2004. *The Meaning of Wife.* New York: Farrar, Straus and Giroux.

Kinsey, Alfred C., Wardell B. Pomeroy, and Clyde E. Martin. 1948. Sexual Behavior in the Human Male. Philadelphia: W. B. Saunders Co.

Kipnis, Laura. 2003. *Against Love: A Polemic.* New York: Vintage Books.

———. 2006. *The Female Thing: Dirt, Sex, Envy, Vulnerability.* New York: Pantheon Books.

Kolata, Gina. 2007. The myth, the math; the sex. *New York Times,* "Week in Review," 12 August.

Krasnow, Iris. *Surrendering to Marriage*. New York: Hyperion Books, 2002.

Lloyd, Carol. I want you so bad. Salon.com, www.salon.com.

Lute, Miriam Axel. And baby makes four: My daughter has two moms, one dad, and no complaints. Babble.com, www.babble.com.

Mann, Dave. 2002. They do, they do: The polygamy world is proliferating via the Internet—especially in Texas. *Fort Worth Weekly,* 30 May, www.fwweekly.com.

McQuade, Donald, and Robert Atwan, eds. 2003. *The Writer's Presence: A Pool of Readings.* New York: Bedford/St. Martin's.

Melly, Diana. 2005. I have an open marriage but there are limits, Jude. *Independent,* 24 July.

Mitchell, Stephen A. 2002. *Can Love Last?* New York: W.W. Norton & Company.

Montandon, Mac. 2007. Are you really satisfying your wife? Men. style.com, 4 September, http://men.style.com/details.

Morford, Mark. 2005. Sex and the disgruntled teen. SF Gate, 25 February, www.sfgate.com.

Newitz, Annalee. 2006. Love unlimited: the polyamorists. *New Scientist* magazine, 7 July, 44.

New York Times. 1854. Growth of Infidelity in the United States, 9 August, http://spiderbites.nytimes.com/articles/free/free185408_3.html.

O'Neill, George, and Nina O'Neill. 1972. *Open Marriage: A New Life Style for Couples.* New York: Avon Books.

Paglia, Camille. 1991. *Sexual Personae: Art and Decadence from Nefertiti to Emily Dickinson.* New Haven, CT: Yale University Press.

Perel, Esther. 2006. *Mating in Captivity.* New York: HarperCollins.

Polyamorous Percolations. 2007. Making an open marriage work, 21 September, www.polyinthemedia.blogspot.com.

Queen, Carol. 1997. *Real Live Nude Girl: Chronicles of Sex-Positive Culture.* Pittsburgh, PA: Cleis Press.

Rich, Adrienne. 1985. Compulsory heterosexuality and lesbian existence. In *Blood, Bread, and Poetry: Selected Prose 1979–1985.* New York: W.W. Norton & Company.

Rosenberg, Debra. 2007. (Rethinking) gender. *Newsweek,* 21 May, 50–57.

Scruton, Roger. 2003. The moral birds and bees: Sex and marriage, properly understood. *National Review,* 15 September, www. nationalreview.com.

Sessions Stepp, Laura. 2006. Cupid's Broken Arrow, Washington Post, 7 May, D01.

Siegel, Deborah. 2007. *Sisterhood, Interrupted: From Radical Women to Girls Gone Wild.* New York: Palgrave Macmillan.

Sprinkle, Annie. The Sex Addiction Myth, www.anniesprinkle.org/html/writings/sex_addiction.html.

Stanley, Alessandra. 2007. Say, darling, is it frigid in here? *New York Times,* 19 August.

Syfers, Judy. 1972. Why I Want a Wife, Ms. magazine, 144.

Talese, Gay. 1995. *Thy Neighbor's Wife.* New York: Ivy Books, the Ballantine Publishing Group.

Taormino, Tristan. 2002. Sex nerds. *Village Voice,* 24–30 April.

Than, Ker. 2006. Scientists Study Factors Behind Fidelity, MSNBC, 20 November, www.msnbc.msn.com.

The Oprah Winfrey Show. 2007. 237 reasons to have sex, 25 September.

Uygur, Cenk. 2007. We're all gay. AOL News, 28 June, http://news. aol.com.

Valenti, Jessica. 2007. *Full Frontal Feminism: A Young Woman's Guide to Why Feminism Matters. Berkeley, CA: Seal Press.*

Vaughan, Peggy. *Who has Affairs—and Why, DearPeggy.com, http://www. dearpeggy.com/affairsmenu.html.*

Wall Street Journal. 2007. The difficulty of counting divorces, 21 May, http://online.wsj.com/public/us.

Warren, Nancy. 2001. I want to try everything once, SF Gate, 26 January, www.sfgate.com.

Weesner, Theo. 2007. The woman I couldn't have. *Glamour,* August, 128–30.

Yalom, Marilyn. 2001. *A History of the Wife.* New York: HarperCollins.

selected online resources

www.4thefamily.us

www.lovemore.com

www.outrageousintimacy.com

www.planetwaves.net

www.polyamory.org

www.polyamoryonline.org

www.polyamorysociety.org

www.polychromatic.com

http://polyinthemedia.blogspot.com

www.polymatchmaker.com

www.practicalpolyamory.com

www.spiritualpolyamory.com

www.tfproject.org

www.zeromag.com/fvpolylinks.html

acknowledgments

I want to thank Seal Press for being courageous enough to take on this project, and Rachel Kramer Bussel for helping them find me. I want to thank my editor, Brooke Warner, for working tirelessly with me every step of the way, no matter how painful some of those steps turned out to be. I want to thank my husband for loving me and allowing me the time and space required to write a book. And I want to thank my daughter for her hugs and kisses and patience. I want to thank Jemma, who inspired me, pushed me, guided me, and saved me about a thousand times through this process. I want to thank my family for all of their love and, specifically, my sister for listening (endlessly and thoughtfully), my father for brainstorming and being my faithful research assistant (read: typist), and my mother for remaining calm (for the most part).

I want to thank all of the Wild Writer Women of Nimrod Hall for always being there for me; Charlotte Morgan and Cathy Hankla (our fearless leaders) for reminding me that the work must be done; the staff and guests for their support; and Frankie and Jimmy Apistolas for giving me a place to renew my body and rekindle my spirit every year. I want to thank Andrea Horton and Tonya Rogers for standing by me without falter. I want to thank Scott Whittal and the entire crew at my favorite coffee shop, Buli, for letting me "office" there for nearly a year. I want to thank *Tango* magazine for publishing and *The Huffington Post* for running "Portrait of an Open Marriage," the piece that led me to this book. I want to thank each person who took the time to fill out a survey for me or respond to my writing online. And I want to thank everyone whose stories and writing and research informed my work all along the way.

I also want to thank Jimmy Belasco, my spiritual advisor, for grounding me and reminding me that the universe provides (all I have to do is be still enough to hear what it is offering); Geoff Shandler for all of his sage advice; Erika Buentello for my gorgeous website and stationary; Jessica Valenti for allowing me to guest blog on Feministing.com; Scogin Mayo for my gorgeous author photo; Gigi Coker and Rose Mariano for making me feel gorgeous in that photo; my publicist Andie East for all of the amazing work she did to get this book out there; and Big J for her open mind, open arms, and open heart. Thank you to all of my friends, family members, and colleagues who supported me and believed in me and loved me. This book belongs to all of us.

about the author

jenny block is a freelance writer
whose work has appeared in a variety of regional and
national publications, including *American Way, Cosmopolitan*
(Germany), *Spirit, The Dallas Morning News, Dallas Voice,
Bee, bRILLIANT, People Newspapers, Where, D, D Home,
Dallas CEO, Stone, Pointe, Virginia Living, Style Weekly,*

Tango, R Health, and *Richmond* magazine. Her online work includes pieces for HuffingtonPost.com, ElleGirl.com, LiteraryMama.com, Chow.com, and PoshCravings.com. In addition, she's contributed essays to *It's a Girl: Women Writers on Raising Daughters* (Seal Press, 2006) and *Letters to My Teacher* (Adams, 2005). She also serves as the senior travel editor for *Stone Magazine.*

Jenny holds both her bachelor's and her master's degrees in English from Virginia Commonwealth University, where she taught composition for nearly ten years. She also spent time teaching at both the University of Richmond and Strayer University, writing and lecturing about teaching and learning for the *Newsweek* Education Program and writing academic ancilliaries for Addison Wesley Longman. She lives with her family in what is affectionately referred to as "the South."

selected titles from seal press

For more than thirty years, Seal Press has published groundbreaking books. By women. For women. Visit our website at www.sealpress.com, and our blog at www.sealpress.com/blog.

ABOUT FACE: WOMEN WRITE ABOUT WHAT THEY SEE WHEN THEY LOOK IN THE MIRROR, edited by Anne Burt and Christina Baker Kline. $15.95, 1-58005-246-0. 25 women writers candidly examine their own faces—and each face has a story to tell.

FULL FRONTAL FEMINISM, by Jessica Valenti. $15.95, 1-58005-201-0. A sassy and in-your-face look at contemporary feminism for women of all ages.

3o SECOND SEDUCTION: HOW ADVERTISERS LURE WOMEN THROUGH FLATTERY, FLIRTATION, AND MANIPULATION, by Andrea Gardner. $ 14.95, 1-58005-212-6. Marketplace reporter Andrea Gardner focuses on the many ways that advertising targets women and how those ads affect decisions, purchases, and everyday life.

HE'S A STUD, SHE'S A SLUT AND 49 OTHER DOUBLE STANDARDS EVERY WOMAN SHOULD KNOW, by Jessica Valenti. $13.95, 1-58005-245-2. With sass, humor, and aplomb, *Full Frontal Feminism* author Jessica Valenti takes on the obnoxious double standards women encounter every day.

OFFBEAT BRIDE: TAFFETA-FREE ALTERNATIVES FOR INDEPENDENT BRIDES, by Ariel Meadow Stallings. $15.95, 1-58005-180-4. Part memoir and part anecdotal how-to, *Offbeat Bride* is filled with sanity-saving tips, advice, and stories to guide even the most out-there bride.

WE DON'T NEED ANOTHER WAVE: DISPATCHES FROM THE NEXT GENERATION OF FEMINISTS, edited by Melody Berger. $15.95, 1-58005-182-0. In the tradition of *Listen Up,* the under-thirty generation of young feminists speaks out.